To the memory of Alan Coleman Batchelder

BATCHELDER
■ TILEMAKER ■

ROBERT WINTER

Balcony Press □ Los Angeles

First Printing

Published in the United States of America
1999

Design by Kurt Hauser
Imaging and production by Navigator Press,
Pasadena, California
Printed in Hong Kong

Batchelder Tilemaker ©1999 Robert Winter

Library of Congress CCN 98-074948
ISBN 1-890449-03-2

CONTENTS

THE DIGNITY OF LABOR

IS OF THE MIND AND HEART,

NOT OF THE HAND ALONE.

FOREWORD

The importance of Ernest Batchelder as an Arts and Crafts tilemaker cannot be overstated. For his innovation in design, his entrepreneurial spirit, his living his life true to the principles that he espoused, he is a man to be admired by all generations.

A hundred years ago, when Ernest Batchelder first became intrigued with tiles, the myths of medievalism were at the core of the Arts and Crafts movement. The Middle Ages provided a grand arena of ideas, customs and practices, both real and imagined, to be revered, albeit from afar, as a time when the artisan had a personal, hands-on relationship with his craft, and master craftsmen were among the most venerated members of society.

For centuries the principles of this earlier "golden age" were carried forth by the brotherhood of Freemasons, a group to which Batchelder belonged, whose members recognized a connection between the quality of workmanship amid high moral standards exemplified by the ancient guilds and the harmony that universal and cosmic laws brought to everyday life. It is within this context that one can appreciate this enterprising young man who, in 1908, left the security of a prestigious teaching position to start his own school, soon to focus on tile making as his medium for self-expression.

The appeal of things medieval was a rejection of the dehumanizing practices and byproducts of the Industrial Revolution. This longing for a more personal and meaningful experience in the workplace was reinforced by the various Arts and Crafts societies that were springing up in urban centers throughout the United States, espousing ideas that would have a direct influence on both the architecture and interior design of the period.

From his early association with Denman Ross, one of the founders of the Boston Society of Arts and Crafts, through his final summer at the Handicraft Guild in Minneapolis, together with his two trips to Europe, Batchelder was engaged in intense self-examination, strengthening his determination to direct his own life. Of critical importance to his career was his early discovery of the tiles of Henry Chapman Mercer of Doylestown, Pennsylvania. Many years later Batchelder would acknowledge Mercer as "the greatest of all American potters...300 years out of his time, probably the only modern artist retaining the glorious touch of the medieval masters." It was this initial encounter that planted the seeds that would come to life and blossom "in a Pasadena garden under the shade of the olive trees."

The inspiration that Batchelder derived from Henry Mercer is undeniable; after all, he chose to accent his own home with Mercer tiles. Although the appearance of Batchelder's tiles bore little resemblance to those of his mentor, each man's tiles represented radical departures from the norm. Like Mercer, Batchelder chose to make his tiles by hand, at least initially, and to allow the "handmadeness" of each tile to remain apparent. The work environment, "a wholesome place in which to work" as Batchelder put it, was as important as the process of production; fellow workers were viewed more as family members than employees. Perpetuators of myth, both men chose similar subject matter for their figure tiles—castles, knights on horseback, ships, folk heroes, minstrels, entwined birds and vines—often derived from medieval symbols and themes. Perhaps most importantly, each man viewed his final products as things of beauty, rather than as strictly utilitarian.

The aesthetic of the fireplace, to which many of these early tiles were destined, was in transition at the time, altered certainly by the introduction of these handcrafted tiles, but also in its composition. Whereas during the Victorian era tiles were most often used sparingly as a single course around the fireplace opening, tiles were now being used for the first time to cover the entire face of the mantel and the hearth as well. Batchelder fittingly wrote, "A fireplace, in a peculiarly intimate sense, is the center of the home. It is the focal point in any scheme of decoration."

The craftsman-style bungalow with its dark, rich interior provided a comfortable environment for the large mantel, an ideal setting for Batchelder's muted, rustic-looking tiles, "luminous and mellow in character, somewhat akin to the quality of a piece of old tapestry." The distinctive, earthy look, blending so harmoniously with the popular interior, conveyed a message of warmth and security, encouraging contemplation and inspiration from the romanticized medieval imagery. With the burgeoning growth in population and the resultant demand for tile in the home, Batchelder-Wilson was propelled to a place of prominence in Southern California and far beyond. In the years that followed, there would be others—Claycraft Potteries, Muresque Tiles, and California Art Tile among them—that would emulate Batchelder's work. Each of these competitors established a reputable and distinctive product line, but none would surpass Batchelder in volume, diversity, or quality of design. Batchelder remained the preeminent leader of handmade tiles in the West until the effects of the Great Depression resulted in the closure of his operations in 1932.

It should be noted that throughout his career as a tile maker, Batchelder was as innovative in his marketing as he was in his design—a mythmaker with a practical inclination. He published his first product catalog, modest though it was, in 1912, a second in 1916, and a third in 1920, before diversifying and producing multiple catalogs throughout the 1920s, each focusing on a separate product— handmade tiles, fountains, pavements, mantels, etc.—all catering to the architectural community. The company's prolific advertising campaign presented the tiles as "eloquently expressive," "remarkably versatile," "primarily artistic in their conception," "the medium through which beauty may be made a thing of permanence." It made ordering of his tiles easy for tile contractors, the principal sales-people for manufacturers in those days, by number-ing individual tile and trim pieces and providing detailed drawings, as well as thorough instructions for installation, to meet each customer's specific needs. By 1925, Batchelder-Wilson had showrooms in Los Angeles and New York, by the end of the decade exclusive showrooms in Chicago and San Francisco as well as representation in virtually every major city in the United States.

Ernest Batchelder's emergence from humble beginnings to become a successful businessman and a pillar of his community whose legacy remains for us to learn from and enjoy is a story in the classic American style. Those among us who appreciate fine craftsmanship can imagine the glow of a crack-ling fire on those mellow earthenware tiles and reflect upon the ideals that guided this man's remarkable life.

Joseph A. Taylor
Tile Heritage Foundation

PREFACE

My interest in Ernest was first stirred by reading his many articles in Gustav Stickley's magazine, *The Craftsman*. One especially delighted me. In 1905 he had visited the great English Arts and Crafts leader Charles Robert Ashbee at the Cotwolds town of Chipping-Campden and found that Ashbee's experiment with hand industry was not working. When Batchelder got home, he wrote an article entitled "Why the Handicraft Guild at Chipping-Campden Has Not Been a Business Success," which included the deathless sentence: "Cooperation that does not cooperate breeds discontent among those who are cooperated upon." It seemed to me that there was little more to say, and I became a Batchelder convert.

My purchase of Batchelder's house in 1972 clinched my conversion. Ernest actually may have designed this wonderful Arts and Crafts place. It is dark inside, but maybe that is as it should be in Southern California, where the sun shines so resolutely. It is a virtual museum of the tile he created from 1910 to 1932. The color becomes more vivid toward the rear of the house and contin-

Ernest Allen Batchelder,
c. 1918.

ues into the backyard and the old kiln house that I have turned into a gallery of Batchelder ceramics. In the guest house next to the garage there is some Spanish Colonial Revival tile and even a little Art Deco.

This book began as a dual biography of Ernest Batchelder, designer and tile maker, and his wife. I had in mind the famous nineteenth-century intellectual team of Harriet Taylor and her husband, John Stuart Mill. I had planned to interweave the Batchelders' lives in a story of mutual support and understanding. Unfortunately, my study did not turn out as I expected. No question, it was a fine marriage, but neither mate was deeply interested in what the other was passionate about. Alice lived for music, and her preoccupation with it kept her from involvement in her husband's work, about which she knew literally nothing. And although Ernest enjoyed music, he never played a musical instrument or sang. In fact, their son, Alan, suggested to me that his father's reputation for being reserved was probably based on the fact that his mother's guests always talked about music and, when his father had had enough, he retired to his study or shop.

Finding much information of a personal nature about the Batchelders has been difficult. They were both raised in a genteel culture that frowned on opening your heart, even in the privacy of your letters. Speaking of family gatherings, Alan wrote, "Effective communication came with difficulty, and most of that at parent-son level was conveyed by my mother." Alan and his father occasionally went on camping trips together when the boy was old enough to enjoy them. But though he was a doting father when his son was a child, Ernest became, and remained, somewhat distant when Alan matured. Fleshing Ernest out has also been difficult because, as Alan told me, his father burned his correspondence with Alice a couple of days after her death in 1948.

Ernest Batchelder may not have oozed charm or been a colorful character, but he gave magnificent color to other people's lives. As I write at Alice's desk, the sound of music sings through the house even when I turn off my phonograph, which now must substitute for her beautiful Steinway.

Batchelder's design for his house used the dark-shingled, Swiss-chalet style we now call "Craftsman" to harmonize with its sylvan setting.

Ernest was a doting, if reserved, father to son Alan

ARTS AND CRAFTS APPRENTICE

1875–1910

Through his writings on design and his prolific production of decorative ceramic tiles from 1910 to 1932, Ernest Batchelder was recognized in his own time as a major contributor to the American Arts and Crafts movement. The broad outlines of his life are clear but many details remain obscure; few of his personal papers have surfaced. Even the year of his birth is in question. It is listed on insurance papers as January 22, 1876, a date that his son, Alan, believed was correct, although almost all other references indicate 1875.[1] Ernest did try to get a copy of his birth certificate from officials of Nashua, New Hampshire, the closest large community to Francestown, the village where he lived until the age of eight. They wrote back that there was no record of his birth in the town archives.

It is possible that he was born at the family home in Francestown, where a formal birth certificate would not have been issued

Thanks to the Batchelder genealogy we know something of his family background. He had solid New England roots. The American Batchelder (also spelled Bachelor) family came to Massachusetts Bay Colony in 1636. Joseph Bachelor was a tailor with some means for he brought three servants with him. Ernest's great-great grandfather, Amos Batchelder, fought in the Revolutionary War after which he settled the family in Francestown. Ernest's father, Charles Levi, was a contractor there.

Batchelder's early life was unhappy, according to his son. The designer's mother, Mary Ann Sleeper, died three years after he was born, and when his father remarried in 1897, the boy was sent to Nashua to live with an uncle. The absence of both parents in his youth was difficult enough, but his uncle, a carpenter, evidently worked him relentlessly. Alan Batchelder remembers that when his father recalled his early years working with his uncle, it was with some bitterness at the long hours of hard work sanding floors and doing other chores.[2] Whatever its rigors, this apprenticeship determined that the initial stages of his career as a craftsman would be based on practical experience not theory.

The prospects for a young New Englander with very little money were not good. Although New England still had a thriving economy after the Civil War, clouds were gathering on the horizon. As one American historian of the postwar period noted, "This historic industrial area was conducting essentially a holding operation."[3] The great industrial expansion after the war was in the Midwest, while only a few industries in New England were growing. In fact, by the 1890s the shift of the cotton industry toward the South foreshadowed New England's ultimate economic decline. Nashua was a factory town that produced textiles. Ernest's reaction to the economic situation, like that of many other New Englanders with ambition, was to seek upward mobility by training to become a teacher. He left Nashua for Boston in 1893, where he entered the Massachusetts Normal Art Institute, a teacher's college with a strong manual training emphasis. According to Paul Dobbs, archivist of the Massachusetts College of Art, "The Student Accessions 1873 – 1923" shows Batchelder received a diploma in 1899 in drawing, painting, and design, and also a diploma in "methods of teaching and supervising drawing, with special reference to the several grades of the public schools."

After graduation he met Denman W. Ross, a professor of art history at Harvard University. In 1901 Ross, who had also been president of the Boston Society of Arts and Crafts, asked Batchelder to work for him at his Harvard Summer School of Design. The young man accepted the offer and soon became familiar with Ross' theories of design, which eventually formed the basis for his own two books, *The Principles of Design* (1908) and *Design in Theory and Practice* (1910).[4] Ross had also contributed designs for the ceramics of Dedham Pottery, a well-known East Coast plant, which might have indirectly influenced Batchelder's later decision to design and produce decorative tiles.

Still searching for opportunities to improve himself, Batchelder decided to move to California in 1901. After a brief stay in Fresno, he settled in

Pasadena, where he was soon employed as an instructor at the Throop (pronounced "troop") Polytechnic Institute, a prep school and college that combined what was called *sloyd* (Swedish for manual training) with the liberal arts and sciences.[5] Founded in 1891, Throop was a trade school in an era when that was not a pejorative term. Its president, James A. B. Scherer, explained the school's purpose in an essay for *Arroyo Craftsman*, a short-lived (one issue!) little Arts and Crafts magazine published in Highland Park in 1909. In the article

Throop Poyltechnic Institute, Pasadena, California c. 1907.

Clay Modeling room at Throop Polytechnic Institute.

"The Throop Idea," Scherer wrote, "Our theory of education is that it ought to fit men and women to do their actual work in the world, while providing them also with those refined tastes that turn much of the bitter of life into zestful enjoyment."[6] This statement not only encompasses the Arts and Crafts dedication to the wedding of hand, head, and heart but also its attachment to William Morris' belief in the value of general studies rather than specialization, which he regarded as one of the iniquities of modernism. Ironically, it was Throop's eventual capitulation to specialization that would turn it into a great scientific institution—the California Institute of Technology (Caltech)—and, not incidentally, lead to Batchelder's break with it.

He apparently felt great satisfaction at finding a position at a reputable academic institution and began involving himself in community activities. At the same time, seeking recognition, he looked beyond Pasadena. He heard of plans for a large exhibition of contemporary arts and crafts at the Louisiana Purchase International Exposition, which was to open in St. Louis in the summer of 1904, and was disturbed that no California work was going to be shown there.[7] In April of that year he wrote to Frederick Allen Whiting, the exposition's superintendent of applied arts, to deplore this omission. It is possible that he had known Whiting in Boston, where the latter had been secretary of the Society of Arts and Crafts before his work on the St. Louis fair. Batchelder offered to bring together a representative selection from California. He suggested that Whiting include examples of Native American basketry and beadwork and also Mexican leather and drawn work.[8]

If the men did indeed know each other at this point, their acquaintance was only casual; Whiting telegraphed their mutual friend Denman Ross, and asked, "Can I rely upon Ernest Batchelder's judgment to select applied art work from California craftsmen for Art Department?"[9] Ross immediately replied, "Doubtful, his judgment pretty good but not sure..."—an amusing remark given that the articles Batchelder had just written for *The Inland Printer* were explicitly based on Ross' principles of design.[10] Whiting evidently needed a California representative, so he telegraphed Batchelder, "Go ahead with preliminary work."[11] But in a follow-up letter written the same day, he insisted that the young man select only works of the highest quality—advice that Batchelder was careful to heed, according to his letters to Whiting. Whiting asked him to consult Charles Fletcher Lummis and George Wharton James, Southern Californians well known to Bostonians for their expert knowledge of Mexican and Native American crafts.[12] He also asked Batchelder to pick characteristic works by other California crafters and then broadened the assignment to make him responsible for the whole Southwest.

By the end of April, Batchelder had assembled contemporary objects from the Navajo, Hopi, Pima, Pomo, and Tulare tribes. He had trouble with the project because Lummis and another prominent collector, W. D. Campbell, the proprietor of the Curiosity Store in downtown Los Angeles, had recently lent items to another exhibition; the works had been damaged and they would not lend anything unless Batchelder personally accompanied the works to St. Louis, something he felt he could not

Arts Palaces of the Louisiana Purchase International Exhibition

Medal given to Batchelder for his work assembling artifacts from the Southwest for the Louisiana Purchase International Exposition of 1904.

do.[13] In early May he and George Wharton James selected objects from the inventory of a Pasadena shop called The Wigwam. Batchelder, in a scholarly aside, warned Whiting that the best Native American Indian work was not contemporary but had been crafted twenty to sixty years earlier.[14] Also, he found it impossible to get the names of Indian craftsmen and thus was unable to meet one of the fundamental principles of Arts and Crafts exhibitions: the artisan must always be identified.[15]

It was easier for Batchelder to collect representative works by Anglo Americans. He went to Santa Barbara and was referred to the work of Mr. Charles Frederick Eaton.[16] Of Eaton's work, he selected two jewelry cabinets, a brass tea set, an inkstand, a lantern, an iron taperholder, a pearl lamp shade, and several illuminated books.[17] Eaton's daughter, Mrs. Elizabeth Burton, was represented through her work by a leather chest, a leather-and-shell mat, a metal-and-shell lamp shade, a shell tea screen, and several other odd items.[18] He also would send some tooled leather work of Mrs. Isobel Austin, although he did not think it was her best effort.[19]

From Santa Barbara he turned north to San Francisco, where he found the prospects less encouraging since the Arts and Crafts Association there had disbanded. A new one had recently been formed by a man named Orlof Orlow, but it was too soon to expect anything from it. A sample of the bookbinding of Rosa Taussig, a pupil of the English craftsman T. J. Cobden-Sanderson, was sold before Batchelder had a chance to pack it and send it to Whiting.[20] Ten examples of the hand-wrought jewelry of Mrs. M. Mott Smith Byrd of San Francisco and a brass candlestick by "a thorough craftsman," Douglas Van Denburgh of Los Gatos, completed the list of things from California.[21] Strangely there was no mention of anything from Batchelder himself or from the Los Angeles area for that matter.

Batchelder never saw the installation of his selections in St. Louis. He told Whiting that he was too busy "economizing for a year of study in the Arts and Crafts in England and France."[22] But before this adventure another opportunity for recognition presented itself. An alternative to a career at Throop opened up in the fall of 1904 when the Handicraft Guild of Minneapolis was founded. Sometimes Batchelder is cited as one of the founders, but the truth is that he organized its summer school the next year when he developed a curriculum modeled on Denman Ross' summer school at Harvard. A short notice in the May 1905 issue of *The Craftsman* announced that the Minneapolis Summer School would "be directed by Ernest A. Batchelder of Throop Polytechnical [sic] Institute, whose course in composition and design will be the central feature."[23]

The summer schools Batchelder directed through 1909 were noticed by *The Craftsman* and other journals and must have been extremely successful if the testimony of the Iowa regionalist painter Grant Wood is representative. Wood was much influenced by the essays that comprised Batchelder's Principles of Design, printed in installments in *The Inland Printer* in 1904.[24] It is conceivable that he also took a correspondence course from Batchelder. It is doubtful that Wood ever studied directly under Batchelder at the summer school, as Darrell Garwood suggests in his biography of Wood, *Artist in Iowa*.[25]

For Ernest, the Minneapolis experience was a great joy. He wrote to Frederick Whiting that he was "charmed with Minneapolis and the work we have under way." In 1905 he had eighty students in his class: "so many pupils working in a variety of crafts-wood-metal-jewelry-pottery-leather—for which designs must be prepared."[26] He was delighted to report that his work was encouraged "by a discriminating demand from people here in the city." He was even considering moving to Minneapolis. "There is talk of making the school a permanent institution" he wrote, "and the temptation to remain here, or at least to return here after the trip abroad is a strong one indeed."[27]

Copper dining room chandelier based on a Batchelder design produced during the period of his teaching at the Minneapolis Guild of Handicraft. It is in 'Wycroft,' a residence in Osceola, Wisconsin, and could have been crafted by Douglas Donaldson, another teacher at the Guild.

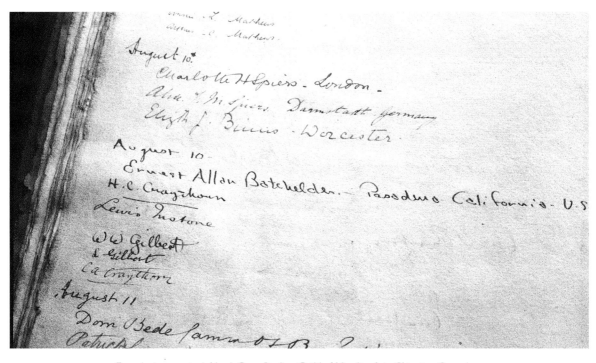

Ernest's signature in Ashbee's Guest Book at Guild of Handicraft in Chipping-Campden.

As this letter suggests, he was planning a trip that would broaden his knowledge of European craftsmanship, ancient and modern. As he planned his European tour, it was obvious that he also intended, while doing research on teaching techniques at craft schools, to educate Europeans on the American phase of the Arts and Crafts movement. He wrote to "Friend Whiting" asking for help in gathering "lantern slides illustrating design and handiwork of our best type, particularly in the lines of ceramics, printing and binding, and metal work....I would like to get some plates to show what

Mercer and Robertson and others are doing."[28] He wrote again in February 1905, saying he looked forward to seeing Whiting in Boston before sailing and to getting photographs of "those stunning things of Mercer" and "two or three of Robertson's plates and vases,"[29] as well as some good examples of eastern printing. He added wistfully, "I wonder if you appreciate your enviable existence—always in Boston!"[30]

He sailed for Europe in the fall of 1905 and first toured Italy, Germany, France, and the Low Countries. He then went to England, "my first love," where he would spend part of the winter at Charles

Sketch by Batchelder of High Street, Chipping-Campden, 1905.

R. Ashbee's experiment in Arts and Crafts cooperation at Chipping-Campden in the Cotswolds.[31]
Ashbee had established the Guild of Handicraft in
East London in the late nineteenth century and had
been successful in turning out beautiful metalwork,
furniture, and jewelry as well as founding the Essex
House Press and using the printing presses that had
once belonged to William Morris.[32] Then in 1901,
during a visit to the United States, Ashbee's wife,
Janet, made an expedition to East Aurora, New
York, to visit Elbert Hubbard and his Roycrofters in
an Arts and Crafts colony sufficiently remote from
Buffalo to permit its inhabitants to practice the simple life.[33] Shortly thereafter, Ashbee's workers voted
to move the guild to Chipping-Campden, one of
the most picturesque towns in the Cotswolds. The
move typified the Arts and Crafts principle of
renouncing the city. As Ashbee, also a friend of
Frederick Whiting, wrote to the Bostonian: "Of
course you must get out into the country as quickly
as you can. These great towns [e.g., London] are a
curse, though you do not feel it as much as we do
because you have got more room to move about."[34]
No doubt the remark seemed gratuitous to Whiting,

Ashbee's move of the Guild of Handicraft from London to Chipping-Camden typified the Arts and Crafts principle of renouncing the city.

who was surely aware that Boston was no London.

Batchelder went to work in the guild shops at Chipping-Campden, where he apparently studied metal working, enameling, and damascene work. He observed that his colleagues were all Londoners who enjoyed the rural idyll during the summer but who seemed bored during the long months of winter. Nevertheless, he admired their workmanship and the freedom Ashbee gave them. "I fear that it would be hard to duplicate them in America," he wrote to Whiting. "They are thoroughly skilled technically and have opportunities to exercise considerable judgment in working out designs."[35]

While at Campden, Batchelder visited the William Morris shrines at Merton Abbey and Morris' grave at Kelmscott. Like many critics, he was sad that the spirit of Morris had apparently died with the Master. He found Morris' old workmen had "finished a tapestry from a design left by [Edward] Burne-Jones and are doing some very bad stained glass, bad in design at least."[36] But his most pungent criticism was in his analysis of Ashbee's problems. The guild's remoteness from the city not only caused boredom among the workers but also affected the economic viability of the experiment. The pastoral setting might be romantic, but the exigencies of the contemporary market required that industry be close to cities. The success of the enterprise rested, moreover, on Ashbee's ability to give it direction and leadership. He was a good and generous man but completely lacking in the kind of charisma that made it possible for his friend Frank Lloyd Wright to succeed at a similar experiment at his home Taliesin in Wisconsin. In fact, Ashbee's attempts to lead sometimes alienated his workers from his mildly socialistic model. Observing all of this, Batchelder wrote, "Cooperation that does not cooperate breeds discontent among those who are cooperated upon."[37] He believed that if the guild had abandoned its socialist scheme and adopted sound business principles, it would have been a success, an observation that is particularly interesting in light of Batchelder's committed capitalistic approach to developing his tile industry.

Ernest did some sketching at Campden and then went on to Birmingham, where he studied in the winter and spring terms of 1905-6 at the Central School of Arts and Crafts (founded in 1884-85), England's first municipal art school. When he registered there, he gave as his English address Edgbaston, the fashionable suburb of Birmingham.[38] Precisely what he studied is not known—possibly metalwork, in which he had shown an interest at Chipping-Campden. An article he wrote for *The Craftsman* in 1908 noted the close relationship between the school and Birmingham's iron and steel industry. The teachers were recruited from the factories and thus could give the students lessons based on firsthand experience. Batchelder was delighted that, "in connection with the school, though in a separate building, is a large and very complete Municipal Museum of Fine and Industrial Art."[39] It was this kind of proximity between the fine and useful arts that was still on his mind when he promoted the creation of an art institute in Pasadena in the 1920s and 1930s.

As he studied in Birmingham, he was not sure he would return to Pasadena. In fact, he gave

Minneapolis as his permanent address. He wrote Whiting: "I left Minneapolis with a heavy heart—for all of my inclinations prompted me to remain and buckle down to a problem that appealed to me strongly. But with others dependent on me for support it seemed unwise to throw up such a position as I now have to cast in my lot through an experimental year with the [Minneapolis] Guild."[40] For the same reasons, he "could not, of course, entertain any proposition from the [Boston] Society."[41] His restlessness was somewhat assuaged when he returned from Europe and was made a director of Throop's art department. As he expressed it to Whiting:

"I felt morally bound to remain here at Throop for the coming year. My position was uncertain about a fortnight ago—for we were passing through an acute crisis. But now that the upheaval is over, with a new president [James A. B. Scherer] and a new policy, I find myself somewhere near the top of the heap. All—and more than I asked in the way of salary—equipment—assistance etc.—has been granted—and I shall remain here until things are on a satisfactory basis."[42]

But his life remained unsettled. After only a year in his new and more secure position, he was off to Europe again on a six-month leave of absence to represent Throop at the International Congress of Art Education held in London in 1908. He wrote to Theodore Coleman, his future father-in-law, that "London is a joy, as usual. It seems like old times to jog along on the bus top, eat pork pies and talk English 'as she is spoke'." The International Congress, with its exhibition "on an immense scale in the new buildings of the South Kensington

Museum of Art" (now the Victoria and Albert Museum) was a great success, and he was given more responsibilities as Throop's representative there.[43]

As he did on his earlier sojourn, Batchelder also toured Europe:

"Have just bought a new wheel—England's best—fully equipped for a continental tour, and leave August 12th, for France. Shall ride through Normandy, Brittany, up the Loire, and down the Rhone to the Mediterranean. Am going to visit many industrial schools afterwards—Zurich, Vienna, Prague, Budapest, Magdeburg, Berlin, etc. I am under contract with The Craftsman Magazine people to write exclusively for them and shall be busy gathering material for this work for two or three months."[44]

At least the French part of this ambitious program was accomplished. The articles on French architecture and crafts appeared in *The Craftsman* in 1909 and were remarkable for Batchelder's beautifully rendered drawings, which recorded a depth of experience that would be valuable to the young craftsman.[45] Certainly this European odyssey must have encouraged his fascination with medievalism.

In announcing Ernest's imminent return to Pasadena in May 1909, the *Pasadena Daily News* referred to him as "formerly the head of the art department at Throop."[46] While in Europe, he had decided to make the final break with the school, a move that reflected his ambition and his abiding determination to pursue new projects. But something else may have affected his decision to give up Throop in order to develop his own school of arts and crafts and establish his own business in tile design and production. It had to do with Throop's changing educational outlook.

In the nineteenth century educators had regarded training in manual arts as being comparable to the sciences and liberal arts. But by the early twentieth century, this perspective on "shopwork" or "the industrial arts" had changed. Increasingly, "manual training" was associated with the inferior status of the working class, whose members, according to popular opinion were not qualified for "higher" education in the liberal arts and sciences and thus had to be groomed for factory labor. The new power of this prejudice, combined with a new emphasis on professionalism, irrevocably altered Throop, where the old idea of a broad, general education was gradually exchanged for specialization in the sciences. Ironically, this change, which had eliminated training in the manual arts, was largely orchestrated by George Ellery Hale, an astronomer, a civic leader in the arts and a person with whom Batchelder would later be closely associated.

Equally ironic is the fact that this specialization at Throop, which caused Batchelder to leave his job, would lead to his own narrowing of interests and finally to his specializing in the design and manufacture of tiles. The first step was his decision to establish a school independent from Throop. After Batchelder returned from Europe in 1909, the *Pasadena Daily News* wrote that en route he had stopped in Boston and secured financial backing of $100,000 for an art school that would be the largest such institution in the country. According to this account, his agents had already purchased a five-acre site overlooking the Arroyo Seco for a new building that would house departments of handicraft and architecture. It added, "During the winter season it is planned to conduct a school especially designed for tourists."[47]

Unfortunately, most of this report seems to have been conjecture. Batchelder, then teaching for the last time in the Summer School at the Handicraft Guild of Minneapolis, immediately disavowed the major details and joked that if a man from Boston had actually given $100,000 "someone sit on him hard and hold him until I can get home, for his presence would clear away a number of bothersome details."[48] But in fact, he was doing some planning:

"I shall open in October a productive workshop and school along the lines of the work done at the Handicraft Guild in Minneapolis with which I have been associated for five years. It is my belief that the conditions in Pasadena are more promising for the success of such an institution than in Minneapolis. In the shops works will be executed in copper and silver, jewelry, enameling, leather and pottery. It is proposed to give special attention to handwrought articles for purposes of home furnishing and at all times to market the product at a minimum price consistent with thoughtful designs and fine workmanship. The enterprise is not primarily for profit, though indeed, it must furnish a decent living to those engaged in the work.

"On the education side, it is intended to follow closely the activities of the shopwork. Provision will be made for those who desire to give serious attention to crafts work as a means of livelihood, either through teaching or practice of a definite craft.

Batchelder's drawing of his house was published in the *Pasadena Daily News* in 1909. The structure was described as a six-room, one story frame bungalow costing $2,600.

There will also be classes for those who have a purely amateur interest in the handicrafts. The craft principle of teaching will be followed in much the same way that we have developed in our education work here, and which has been so successful in attracting serious workers to our summer school."[49]

Interestingly, a similar idea had already been tried a few miles down the Arroyo Seco by George Wharton James, sometime associate editor of *The Craftsman*, and William Lees Judson, a painter who founded the School of Fine Arts at the University of Southern California. They called it the Arroyo Guild of Fellow Craftsmen, and it was in the Guild's journal that James A. B. Scherer championed the "Throop Idea"—the very idea that Batchelder was now forsaking by specializing in the arts and crafts.[50]

In September 1909 Batchelder bought a piece of land on Arroyo Drive (now South Arroyo Boulevard) half a block south of its intersection with California Street, and applied for a permit to construct a bungalow.[51] The permit for the house is dated September 8, 1909. The structure was described as a six room, one story frame bungalow costing $2600. Originally, it was supposed to be a single story, but even before construction began the plan was modified to provide a bedroom and a sleeping porch on the second floor.[52] Batchelder was likely the designer, although he may have had the help of an architect—perhaps Louis B. Easton, who designed several houses nearby.[53] Batchelder's drawing of the proposed facade was published in the *Pasadena Daily News*.

This ceramic medallion of Batchelder's personal insignia of a rabbit sketching originally hung in front of his house.

Except for the treatment of the front window, it was precisely what we see in the completed structure. He chose the dark-shingled, Swiss-chalet style we now call "Craftsman" that would harmonize with its sylvan setting under great oaks that cast their shadows on the red composition sheeting of the roof. The prominent chimney on the front elevation was set on a foundation of clinker bricks and arroyo boulders that joined the house with its natural surroundings.

Batchelder expressed his interest in the tile work of Henry Mercer by installing various examples of it around the house, especially on the chimney, where he inserted numerous pieces from his collection. He

Handworked copper detailing by Douglas Donaldson in Arts and Crafts themes is represented in the mailbox and front door hardware.

Batchelder's 1909 house on the Arroyo in Pasadena was the original site of his tile making enterprise.

Batchelder's fireplace prior to its redesign.

Batchelder tipped his hat to the accomplishment of Henry Mercer by accenting his own house with Mercer's tiles such as one similar to this mounted on the front door.

Batchelder built a desk off the living room that also served as a display counter. The music cabinet to the right was added later after Ernest married Alice Coleman, an accomplished pianist.

set another large Mercer tile into the metalwork on the heavy redwood front door; it bears a Latin inscription from Psalm 46: "Fluminis impetus letificat civitatem dei." (There is a river, the streams whereof shall make glad the City of God.) A number of years ago Linda Dyke, in doing research on the Moravian Pottery and Tile Works at Doylestown, Pennsylvania, discovered a bill of lading for twenty-four tiles shipped to Batchelder on July 30, 1907. Eleven of these can be found installed in various parts of the house.

The living-room where Batchelder would exhibit his own works and those of his students was paneled in naturally stained redwood and Oregon pine (Douglas fir) up to a frieze beginning about two feet below the low-pitched ceiling. He planned to eventually paint the frieze in scenes from Chaucer's *Canterbury Tales*, with eucalyptus and oaks in the background.[54] He never accomplished the frieze painting or the installation of perforated screens with carved peacocks that he intended for the openings in the staircase. Copper sconces and chandeliers in Batchelder's Birds-in-the-Tree tile pattern were later fabricated by Douglas Donaldson and hung in both the living room and dining room.

At the northeast corner of the living room, where the ceiling was lowered to make room for the upstairs sleeping porch, Batchelder built a desk that also served as a display counter. Dominating the living room was a brick fireplace that prompted the writer for the *Pasadena Evening Star* to observe: "[T]he rough black hearth is inlaid with suggestive tiles [Mercer?] and brasses, which make a long study before a cheerful fire not one of pure musing."[55] In a

View from the dining room to the living room. None of the furniture is original.

The beautifully tiled porch, was where Batchelder's wife, Alice, would keep the silent keyboard she used to strengthen her fingers.

wing jutting off at a right angle to the south was the dining room, also paneled in dark redwood and Oregon pine but much brighter than the living room because French doors, with panes set horizontally to suggest shoji screens, dominated the west wall. Later, a bay window was added on the south wall, probably to admit more light.

Beyond the dining room was an unfinished room, probably a porch or fernery, which was later beautifully tiled. Here Batchelder's wife, Alice, would keep the silent keyboard she used to strengthen her fingers.

In November 1910, Ernest obtained a permit to construct a shed for $300 in the back yard.[56] Now he could finally set up a shop and school for the students he brought with him from Throop. Soon this structure would house a single kiln and become "The Birthplace" of Batchelder's new profession: tile making.

In 1910 Ernest set up a shop and school behind his house. Soon this structure would house a single kiln and become "The Birthplace" of Batchelder's new tile making enterprise.

THEORY AND PRACTICE

1910–1925

Somewhere in this period of teaching, traveling, house building, and general self-discovery, Batchelder found time to compile two books: *The Principles of Design*, published first in installments in 1904 and then as a book in 1908 by *The Inland Printer*, and *Design in Theory and Practice*, which first appeared as a series of articles in *The Craftsman* (1907–8) and was then published by Macmillan in 1910. In the preface to *Principles*, which was written for people interested in the graphic arts, the author acknowledges his debt to Denman W. Ross, the professor who had given him a job in 1901.

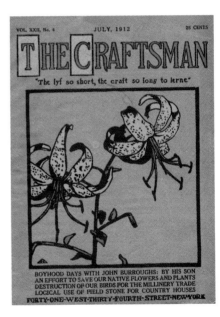

A 1912 copy of *The Craftsman*, which originally published Batchelder's book *Design in Theory and Practice* as a series of articles in 1907 and 1908.

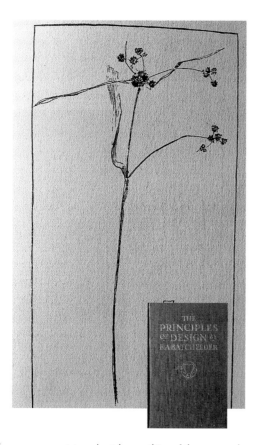

"If you can appreciate and catch something of the grace and beauty of line in a simple wayside weed, nature will yield you more in the way of suggestions for further work than if you sit down to the joyless task of torturing some gorgeous hothouse flower into conventional lines." EAB *The Principles of Design*

A reviewer once remarked that Batchelder's "theories are based on sound study and he writes with the directness of an active worker."

Batchelder notes that the reader who knows Ross' work will, "recognize at once a development from his ideas .... It is from this association [with Ross] that I date my present interest and enthusiasm in the theory and practice of design."[1]

The Principles of Design focuses on practice. It is a didactic textbook of theory leading to a declaration of the laws governing good design. Of particular interest are the eclectic illustrations that are intended to be examples of good—and occasionally bad—design. Batchelder did most of the line drawings, some of which resemble illustrations that he found in Arthur Wesley Dow's manual, *Composition: A Series of Exercises in Art Structure for the Use of Students and Teachers*, (1899, revised 1913). Dow's book was a staple of American art education in the early twentieth century. In his book *Renegade Regionalists*, James M. Dennis traced Dow's ideas through the theory of Denman Ross to Batchelder whom he sees as a major force in advancing abstraction in American modernist painting.[2]

One figure (Plate XXII) illustrates the geometries Batchelder considered necessary to achieve balance in an asymmetrical design. Other illustrations seem to be derived from Islamic designs, and some are

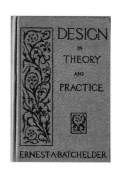

Native American derivations. But the most common sources of what Batchelder considered good design are Japanese prints, impressions of which frequently appear in both books. In *The Principles of Design* Batchelder states, "The American gardener admires symmetry and conscientiously

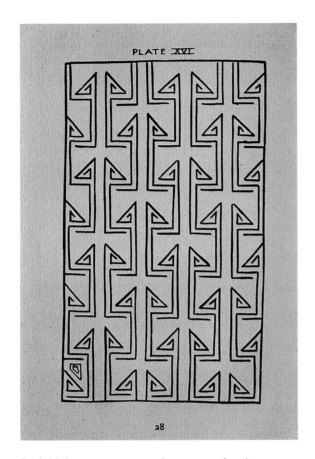

PLATE XVI

28

Batchelder's repetitive geometrical patterns may have been suggested by Froebel kindergarten material.

Alfred Heineman, a Pasadena architect who had taken a Batchelder design course, pointed at Plate XXII and said, "There it is — all Batchelder's theory."

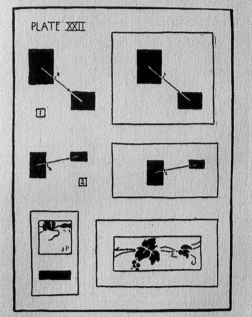

that the point of balance of the measures shall coincide with the center of the frame. Mark that, for it is important. The eye naturally seeks the center of such a frame; it also seeks the point of balance

PLATE XXII

half way between the two measures, hence we should see that the center of the one coincides with the balance point of the others. Figs. 2, 3 illustrate the same problem, the shape of the enclosing form being

The most common sources of what Batchelder considered good design are Japanese prints,
impressions of which frequently appear in both volumes.

prunes his trees accordingly. The Oriental gardener recognizes nature's higher law and aids her to attain the type of balance for which she strives."

Because *Design in Theory and Practice* was written for *The Craftsman*, Batchelder attempted to appeal to a broader audience than those who read *Principles*. As a result, the text is quite general except in sections called "Problem" where he takes the reader through step-by-step exercises to demonstrate a design principle.

Batchelder believed that art has its origin in function, an idea that was being aired at the same time by Louis Sullivan in his theories of architecture and John Dewey in his aesthetics. Like Dewey, Batchelder perceived that in the process of creation, what he called "The Play Impulse," takes over and the artist's imagination is let loose.[3] His statement in the context of the time shows his awareness of an issue affecting most artistic disciplines.

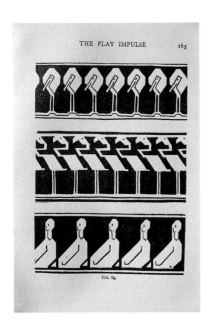

FIG. 89.

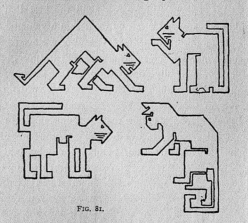

purpose to seek a happy middle ground between
Nature and the geometric basis on which the work ha
developed, to retain the distinctive character of a nat
ural form without sacrificing the distinctive characte
that claims interest from a design point of view. A

FIG. 81.

reasonable knowledge or observation of animal anatomy
is, of course, essential; with such facts of observation
at hand, together with a spice of imagination and a
sense of humor, the limitations of the squared paper
will be found more interesting than if greater liberty
were allowed. Figure 81 indicates the general character of the results that might be expected from practice

"The Play Impulse" proposes that art begins with functional con-
siderations but that, at some point, pure play takes over and the
artist's imagination is set loose.

"A reasonable knowledge of animal anatomy is, of course, essential; with such facts of observation at hand, together with a spice
of imagination and a sense of humor, the limitations of the
squared paper will be found more interesting than if greater liberty were allowed." EAB

The books received universally favorable
reviews. The critic assessing *The Principles of Design* for
the important journal *International Studio* thought it
was a book "students will find worthwhile mastering
from cover to cover."[4] A reviewer for the same magazine deplored the fact that in *Design in Theory and
Practice*, Batchelder repeated "the old saw that as to
art we are a young country without traditions—a
notion which it is high time someone should can-
didly examine and explore." But he went on to
maintain that the author's "theories are based on
sound study and he writes with the directness of an
active worker."[5] A review in *The Outlook* noted
Batchelder's practical bent and compared *Design in
Theory and Practice* to Sadakichi Hartmann's recently
published *Landscape and Figure Composition*.[6] These

Islamic inspired Minton tile in the wall of the choir of the church of St. Giles, Cheadle, England. The church was designed in 1856 by A.N.W. Pugin, a leader in the revival of Catholicism in English church architecture.

reviews and others were mainly summaries of Batchelder's ideas.[7] He was not reviewed in any journal that probed deeply into his aesthetic—probably because it simply was not very deep. His true contribution was his daily teaching, his service to the community, and his exceptional work in tile design and manufacturing.

Batchelder's heart was in design—not in theory. "My father was no intellectual," his son Alan once said. Only when he was in his backyard shack, surrounded by his students intently designing tiles, was he in his element. He never wrote specifically about how he became interested in ceramics, but perhaps he was inspired by the many installations he saw during his European travels.

England, in particular, was experiencing a tile

renaissance in the middle of the nineteenth century. Drawing upon the designs of tiles in medieval churches, Herbert Minton (Minton & Co., later Minton, Hollins & Co.) began mass-producing decorative floor tile in 1840, having purchased a patent allowing him to make tiles from clay dust. Working closely with the architectural community, Minton maintained a virtual monopoly in the floor tile market until Maw & Co. and other companies entered the field some 10 to 15 years later. By that time, tile floors had become the vogue.

The demand was directly related to the Gothic Revival, involving both the restoration of old churches and the construction of an extraordinary number of new ones. As early as the mid-1850s these English tiles were being exported to the United States, a phenomenon that spurred Americans to copy the style. Hyzer and Lewellen of Philadelphia, the Pittsburgh Encaustic Tile Co. in Pittsburgh, and the American Encaustic Tiling Company of Zanesville, Ohio, were among the first to successfully produce tiles of similar quality as early as 1870.[8]

The use of tiles was not limited to churches. In 1878 John Gardner Low founded a tile works in Chelsea, Massachusetts, not to imitate the English but to create his own distinctive pressed tiles, which featured Japanese-style birds and flowers in low relief and high glaze.[9] Often used in fireplace surrounds, these objects, known as "art tiles," figured importantly in the American aesthetic movement.[10]

Batchelder would have been quite aware of this phenomenon, just as he also probably knew that the protean William Morris had designed tiles. And he was already familiar with the American tiles of

successful. In Plate LIV, Fig. 1 shows the divisions of the rectangle. It is generally unwise to associate two or more spaces that are almost but not quite the same in shape and measure. In this case the three spaces in the center of the design are so nearly alike that we feel a desire either to make them just alike or to make them distinctly unlike, as in Fig. 2.

PLATE LV

GRUEBY TILES

GRUEBY FAIENCE COMPANY 2A PARK STREET BOSTON

So, as between these two, we would choose Plate LV as being the better example. At first glance the space here seems to have been divided as in Fig. 1. But a second examination shows that additional charm has been imparted to the work by bringing the word "tiles" into the same width as the middle space. This results in the divisions of Fig. 2. Here we feel the interest, whether we care to analyze the

97

In *The Principles of Design* Batchelder cited advertisements for tiles made by the Grueby Faience Company of Boston in his analysis of good graphics.

This Grueby tile reflects the medievalism popular early in the century.

Henry Mercer of Doylestown, Pennsylvania.[11] In *The Principles of Design* he noted advertisements for tiles made by the Grueby Faience Company of Boston in his analysis of good graphics.[12] It is likely that these sources helped inspire him to become a tile maker, even though he apparently knew more about other crafts than he did about ceramics.

It should also be noted that Batchelder, although a pioneer in the handcrafting of tiles, was not the first tilemaker in Southern California. As early as 1900 an Englishman named Joseph Kirkham trained in ceramics at the Wedgewood factory at Stoke-on-Trent, settled in Tropico (now Glendale), a small city north of Los Angeles and started producing tiles under the company name Pacific Art Tile, later Western Art Tile. The Los Angeles Pressed Brick Company, one of the largest clay products concerns in the state, began crafting tile for fireplaces in 1907. At about the same time that Batchelder began production in his backyard in 1910, other tile companies were starting up. Walter Nordhoff founded

Four musician corbels used at the rear of the Culbertson house (below) by Greene and Greene,1911.

the California China Products Company in National City in 1911, and William Wade opened the Wade Encaustic Tile Company in Vernon in 1912. Obviously there was a demand for art tile, a demand soon fanned by the vogue of the Spanish Colonial Revival that was inspired by the Panama-California Exposition held at San Diego in 1915.[13]

By 1910 Batchelder was producing a small number of handcrafted tiles in only one kiln in his backyard shack. The great Pasadena architects Charles and Henry Greene used Batchelder's four musicians corbels in their Culbertson house of 1911; the fact that these objects are numbered 51, 52, 53, and 54 in his first catalog, issued in 1912, shows that production had started earlier. It is astonishing that Batchelder—with a single kiln and very little tile-making experience—was producing fifty-four patterns by 1911.

For a 1925–26 advertising campaign Ernest wrote "A Little History of Batchelder Tiles" in which he referred to the beginnings of his venture.[14] "Twelve years ago," he recalled, "Batchelder Tiles were made in a Pasadena garden under the shade of the olive trees." The account is so charming that it merits an extensive quote. "The clay was brought home from a brickyard wrapped in gunny sacks, all mixed ready for use. In spite of its humble origin it possessed potential beauty when brought into contact with adequate ideas. We had the ideas and sought to give them expression. We soon went into 'quantity production' by making twelve six-inch tiles at a single process—a commendable bit of enterprise. Our kiln permitted us to fire nearly forty six-inch tiles at one fell swoop. It took three firings to satisfactorily produce our first mantel order. The mantel was laid out on a kitchen floor and personal-

Batchelder rarely dropped a design from his catalog. These tiles were designed very early in his career
but were still being produced in the 1920s.

ly delivered at the job because we had doubts as to
the trustworthiness of expressmen—and, incidentally, feared the owner of the house might change
his mind.

"The olive trees still weave sunlight and shadow
over the roof of the little shop but its activities
remain only as a pleasant memory. The kiln soon
sputtered itself into premature old age—it tried hard
to keep the pace; the neighbors objected to the
soot—and so withal we established ourselves down
among the gas tanks in a galvanized iron shed in
regions remote from neighborly solicitude."[15]

The move to larger quarters, probably made in
1912, to a site on Broadway (now Arroyo Parkway)
indicated the business' success.[16]

Batchelder's early designs for decorative tiles
resembled those he had used to illustrate his two
books on design. His subject matter owed a debt to
Mercer's medievalism: Viking ships, animals, foliage,
scenery, knights, and castles. But the subtlety of
Batchelder's designs and his early predilection for
muted colors and a soft, matte finish distinguished
them from Mercer's "Moravian" tiles. Batchelder's
affinity for Byzantine themes (for instance, pairs of
birds) was more closely related to that of his counterparts in the English Arts and Crafts movement.
Like his contemporary Frank Lloyd Wright, he was
also inspired by Japanese prints, although the effect
on his designs was more in elegance of line than in
actual subject matter.

Batchelder's early designs owed a debt to Mercer's medievalism.

This tile was made quite late in Batchelder's production and shows how his medievalism was sustained throughout his career.

In the early days the predilection was for muted colors and a soft matte finish. These tiles were very understated in a tone that harmonized extremely well with the woodsy Arts and Crafts interiors that were in vogue.

Batchelder's affinity for Byzantine themes was closely related to that of his counterparts in the English Arts and Crafts movement. Compare the stonework of the twelfth-century pulpit at Torcello in Italy to the tile inset on Batchelder's own backyard fountain opposite.

Installation at the Union Automotive Building, Los Angeles.

Except for the passing mention of details in his "Little History" we have no exact description of his production methods. A few years ago, Joseph Taylor, President of the Tile Heritage Foundation, made some speculations based on his experience and on a close examination of Batchelder's works: "Batchelder would first hand-make a model of the tile in soft clay, enlarged proportionately to allow for the clay's ultimate shrinkage during firing. A master or "key" mold would then be cast from this clay tile model. Once the plaster was dry, a fresh impression could be made by pressing malleable clay into the master, from which a production mold would be struck. In turn, the tiles for any particular job would be pressed from the production mold. Depending upon the frequency of its use, a production mold eventually wears out or breaks; the key

Batchelder tiles show a variety of stamps from various periods in the company's history.

Opposite: Tile pattern of the twenties shown after its initial bisque firing and after final glazing.

mold would then be reemployed to create a second impression, from which a new production mold would be made.

Initially, when the clay was pressed into the molds by hand, any excess would be removed by pulling a wire across the top of the mold, thus creating a smooth surface for the back of each tile. At this point, the craftsman would stamp his mark, "Batchelder" etc., into the back of each tile. Once the tiles were dry, or "green" as Batchelder referred to them, the coloring would be applied. The muted and often mottled colors, characteristic of these tiles, were applied by brush or by dipping each tile into a colored slip (engobe) and then wiping it off, probably with a rag or sponge. The duller colors would be applied first and then the brighter colors, the latter ending up in the deeper recesses of the design.

In his own writings, Batchelder implies that his tiles are fired only once, and this may have been the case with his field (undecorated) tiles. Historian Elva Meline wrote in Spinning Wheel, November 1971: "Some tiles were given a bisque firing, then decorated and glazed and refired. Many were decorated before reaching the kiln, especially those with the engobe finish." Marie Glasse Tapp, a practicing tile ceramist advises "...getting the color on the relief tiles requires having bisque to work on. As you apply color, wash off some, apply another color,

wash off some, apply the final color. You couldn't do this working on greenware."[17]

In the early days the predominant colors were various shades of brown. Tiles from this period had a soft, muted surface, very understated, and a tone that harmonized extremely well with the woodsy Arts and Crafts interiors that were in vogue in the early twentieth century. Batchelder wrote:

"Like a Persian rug, our tiles lend themselves to any environment and bring distinction to it. They are hand wrought and possess all the charming little irregularities of shape, size, and texture peculiar to a hand made products. They have a soft finish that mellows with time, free from disagreeable reflected lights so often encountered in tiles. Each tile has individual character; and when set into combinations the result presents a delightful variation of color and form. In fact, it might be said that we do not make tiles! We make fireplaces, each tile a unit in a thoughtful scheme. Each order that comes to our factory is given attention as a fireplace, not so many tiles 'per sample.' The design is laid out on the floor, adjusted to a definite color scheme, and the tiles numbered to fit a key design sent with the shipment."[18]

As this account indicates, his first special work was with fireplaces. "A fireplace," he insisted, "is not a luxury; it is a necessity—because it adds to the joy

Typical early tiles from 1914 and 1918 show characteristic muted brown tones
and subjects from nature.

The more muted colors would be applied first, the brighter colors afterwards which usually ended up in the deeper recesses.

Ornate tiles from the late teens and early 1920s.

and beauty of living." Since it naturally dominates a room, "it must be thought out with a restraint that shall keep it in its proper place as a unit in a harmonious whole. Its proportions, form, and color must always be considered as relative to other things. It should invite attention without being obtrusive; it should quietly assert itself as if to say, 'Look, what measure of comfort and cheer this room affords you.'"[19]

In spite of the custom-made aspect of his fireplaces Batchelder evidently had mastered the art of shipping them to distant locations. Architectural historian Pamela D. Kingsbury of Wichita, Kansas, has discovered fifty-eight Batchelder fireplaces in Kansas, forty-nine of them in the Wichita area. Speculating on why there are so many in an area so far from Batchelder's plant, she suggests that Wichita real estate men such as Alton Smith , who had been interested in land development in

BATCHELDER TILES

{ A Batchelder Mantel of special design, in a
Coronado Home. Elmer Grey, Architect }

"A fireplace," Batchelder insisted, "is not a luxury;
it is a necessity because it adds to the joy and
beauty of living. In fact, it might be said that we
do not make tiles! We make fireplaces, each tile a
unit in a thoughtful scheme."

PERHAPS the greatest virtue, and certainly an
unique one, of Batchelder Tiles, is that they
harmonize with any surroundings. There are no
glaring highlights, no vividly obtrusive colors to
clash with the decorative motif or furnishings.

The joy of installing a distinctive mantel; a lovely
fountain; a beautiful bathroom; pavement or door-
way of Batchelder Tile, is only exceeded by the
splendid results achieved.

See Sweet's Catalogue or write for complete information.

BATCHELDER-WILSON COMPANY
2633 Artesian Street, Los Angeles
101 Park Avenue, New York City

Fireplaces at 248 South Pershing (1920),above, and 201 Riverside (1928), below, in Wichita, Kansas. The earlier example has insets of Batchelder's decorative tiles—a California oak and a medieval castle—that are reworkings of designs illustrated in his first catalog of 1912.

Fireplace Cannon residence, Salt Lake City, Utah. Fireplace (top) location unknown.

Southern California in the early years of the century, were familiar with Batchelder's work and therefore played upon the country's fascination with the Southland to promote sales. Smith's Wichita firm was even called the "California Bungalow Company."

This celebration of the fireplace has a special significance in the context of the social history of the time. In his important study of Frank Lloyd Wright, Robert Twombly detailed the many ways that Wright reinforced the idea of home in an age buffeted by the forces of mobility and modernity, when traditional values seemed under attack. The advantage Wright had, according to Twombly, was his essential conservatism and his oft-repeated suggestion that his houses were havens from a heartless world.[20] Certainly Batchelder's concern for the fireplace was an aspect of his similar search for domesticity.

It was in just this mood of celebrating the home that Batchelder contemplated marriage. Ernest had fallen in love with Alice Coleman, a talented pianist and founder in 1904 of the Coleman Chamber Music Concerts, one of the oldest such organizations in the United States. She is of great significance as a woman who excelled in one of the few fields that was open to women early in the century. Their nephew Ted Coleman believed their relationship may have begun in Boston, where both had studied in the 1890s. Their son, Alan Batchelder, on the other hand, thought they met much later, probably in the early days of

the Music and Art Association, an organization founded in 1911 in order to promote the arts in Pasadena.

One can only speculate upon what attracted them to each other. Like Ernest, Alice had a strong interest in the arts. She must have seen in Ernest an ambitious man, furthermore a successful man, who would support her interest in music even though he knew little about it. Ernest must have been attracted by Alice's agreeable personality upon which her students often remarked. They were married on July 25, 1912, in a ceremony conducted by the Reverend Robert Freeman of the Pasadena Presbyterian Church.[21] Certainly the marriage to Alice changed Ernest's life.

The first indication was a transformation of his bachelor's quarters starting in 1912–13. The house into which Alice moved after the wedding was very much Ernest's, having been designed by him to be a studio as well as a home. Now he set out to make the raftered front room into something that would be more to his wife's liking. It became Alice's studio and classroom. Ernest built a music cabinet for her at the end of the desk he had already constructed. Her magnificent Steinway was placed in front of the north window that looked out to the garden.

The most impressive of several additions and improvements was a new

Alice Coleman Batchelder c. 1910.

As a very personal sign of her husband's affection on each side of the chimney piece two specially designed tile lions were installed. In the shield of the one on the right, Batchelder put his own logo—a rabbit sketching—and in the shield of the one on the left, he placed a harp, representing Alice's musical interests.

Alice and Ernest, both significant contributors to the arts and culture of Pasadena were presented this medal in 1936 with the Arthur Noble Award.

fireplace, possibly a wedding present to Alice, since it seems to have been installed just two months before they were wed.[22] Whatever the occasion and date, it was a very personal sign of her husband's affection. Near the low-pitched ceiling on each side of the chimney piece were two specially designed tile lions that Batchelder modeled on the "Marzocco" figure designed by Donatello for the newel post of a papal apartment in Florence. In the shield of the one on the right, Batchelder replaced the lily of Florence with his own logo—a rabbit sketching—and in the shield of the one on the left, he placed a harp, obviously intended to represent Alice's musical interests. The main body of the fireplace consisted of Batchelder's mottled brown tiles into which were inserted rows of his "Viking ship" design and also some Mercer tiles, possibly salvaged from the earlier fireplace. A frieze above the firebox was composed of the plants and animals that he loved to draw. And in a central panel were large tiles decorated with paired birds in what he called his "Italian" pattern, more than a little reminiscent of Byzantine designs. The superb workmanship and meticulous choice of tiles suggest the special significance of this fireplace.

Most of Batchelder's assignments in these early years were for domestic work—fountains, billiard rooms, front halls and, of

course, fireplaces. What was probably his first large commercial commission, the Dutch Chocolate Shop, allowed him to execute his ideas on a broader scale. In 1914 a developer, noting the great success of the Pig-n-Whistle Restaurant chain, decided to remodel an old building on West Sixth Street in downtown Los Angeles to promote what he hoped would become a fad: hot chocolate. He secured the services of the Los Angeles architectural firm of Plummer and Feil, who apparently suggested that Batchelder be commissioned to do the interior.

Batchelder's model was a kind of German *bierstube*, with arches and vaults covered with tiles. In the rounded panels on the walls were fanciful scenes from Dutch life, and tucked in here and there would be sculptured tiles with similar Dutch themes. Evidently, Batchelder left much of the design to one

of his former Throop students, Anne Harnett, who had now become his most trusted assistant: in fact, some of her relatives remember going to the public library to find books illustrated with Dutch scenes that Harnett could adapt to the project.[23] No doubt Batchelder also participated in the design, which he described in the periodical *Western Architect*.

"The composition, of course, was the first thought. In working out these schemes we made our composition to a small scale, in charcoal, in order to get the massing and space-breaking, utilizing for local details all the data that we could get hold of. Having established the scheme on a small scale we then erected a long board in the studio, which

Batchelder's model for the Dutch Chocolate Shop in downtown Los Angeles was a kind of German bierstube, with arches and vaults, covered with tiles. In the rounded panels on the walls were fanciful scenes from Dutch life, and tucked in here and there were sculpted tiles with similar Dutch themes.

for example, the water line is in about the same relative place in each panel and approximately in the same balance with space and mass."[24] He signed the project by putting "Batchelder Studios" on a Dutch gable in one corner of the large room.

Research to date indicates that the Dutch Chocolate Shop was the only large commission to be fabricated in Pasadena. Its size must have taxed the capacity of the little shop on Broadway, which could barely produce five hundred tiles at a single firing. In fact, the process can only be described as quaint. The bisquets were dried in the sun in the yard behind the main building, "where cats and chickens frequently walked over them offering a pleasing variation of texture." Finally, a somewhat

enabled us to keep two full-sized cartoons going at once. Here cartoons were made plus shrinkage, and were worked up in charcoal and colored crayons with such changes as were necessary in the full size enlargements from the smaller compositions. These cartoons were then traced and further refinements were made in this way, and the tracings were then transferred to full-sized slabs of moist clay. As the slabs were to be cut into smaller units, we established lightly the cutting lines and in transferring the designs to the clay made minor changes to accommodate these units. Each panel was then modeled in three general planes, glazed and fired, each unit being marked with a "key" in order that the panels might be properly assembled when ready for setting. We were not intent upon rendering the actual colors of Holland but had in mind the application of a color scheme to a given problem.

"In cases where a definite bit of architecture has been followed I have found it almost always necessary to change the scheme about in order to keep the continuity throughout the panels. You will note,

Batchelder "signed" the installation with a sculpted mural of a tile studio.

The arches displayed scenes from Holland such as this canal and windmill.

primitive drying room was erected, with a gas stove under tarpaulins providing the heat.[25] Several additions were made to the buildings, but as business boomed, new quarters had to be found.

Certainly the prosperous twenties were the most lucrative for the Batchelder-Wilson Company. Significant was the addition of a business partner, Lucian H. Wilson, who most likely managed the business operations while Batchelder oversaw design and production. In 1920 the company moved to a new factory at 2933 Artesian Street near downtown Los Angeles. At first the business was housed in an

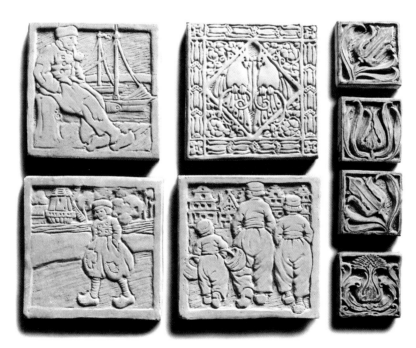

Batchelder delegated much of the design to his assistant, Anne Harnett. Some of her relatives remember going to the public library to find books illustrated with Dutch scenes that Harnett could adapt to the project.

old barn, but it gradually expanded until, as Batchelder wrote in 1925, "We have now seven acres with a plant covering a considerable part of the ground."[26] His staff had increased considerably too—from 4 in 1914 to 175 workers a decade later. By the time the firm had outgrown its Broadway plant, it was using only four kilns of limited capacity. Batchelder was proud of his eleven kilns on Artesian Street. The last to be installed was a continuously generating tunnel kiln that "demands a minimum of 6 tons of material daily."[27] He moved his drafting room from the old kiln house in his backyard, where it had remained after the first move, to a special section of the new quarters. He now had a factory complete with an assembly line.

Devotees of the Arts and Crafts movement will recognize a deviation here from the principles of William Morris. While Morris himself did not shun machinery that could perform work that was odious to the workman, he certainly was not an enthusiast of the machine, perhaps hoping that it would disappear along with the state and the capitalist system.[28] By contrast, early on, Batchelder had written that "Machinery is not in itself an evil; we need more of it." In a characteristic American interpretation of the Arts and Crafts movement, Batchelder wrote, "The evil of machin-

ery is largely a question of whether machinery shall use men or men shall use machinery.... The dignity of labor is of the mind and heart, not of the hand alone."[29]

Batchelder's social principles were not compromised by his mechanized plant, although one of his employees claimed he hired a workman just to scratch the mass-produced tiles with a carborundum stone so he could truthfully advertise, "No two tiles the same,"[30]

As the production increased, taste was, as ever, changing. Sometime around 1922, Batchelder hired a young graduate of the University of Illinois, Ivan Branham, who was a color specialist. Soon after, patterns that had previously been primarily brown

Batchelder and some of his workers at the Artesian Street factory. Linia Jacobus (middle), Emma Clayton and Doris Johnson (top).

By the time the firm had outgrown its Broadway plant, it was using four kilns of limited capacity. Batchelder was proud of his eleven kilns on Artesian Street. The last to be installed was a continuously generating tunnel kiln that "demands a minimum of 6 tons of material daily."

Pool, J.L. Parsons residence, Llewellyn Park, West Orange, New Jersey. Delano & Aldrich Architects.

Main Hall and Stairs, De Pasquale Residence, Pelham Manor, NY. D.A. Summo Architect.

or gray tinged with blue blossomed into greens, oranges, and lavenders.[31] Many new tile patterns emerged, some devised by Batch-elder. But apparently other designers were involved as well. In his "Little History," Batchelder mentions "the sympathetic interpretation of the designs at the hands of Mr. and Mrs. Ingels," who may have contributed directly to the design process. William Manker, who would

become an important ceramist on his own, was employed in the late 1920s; he, too, may have been involved in designing Batchelder tiles.

Some of the patterns that emerged do not seem to be in the style of the man who earlier had produced the designs for his two books. But, personal style can change. Particularly important was a new line of pre-Columbian pat-

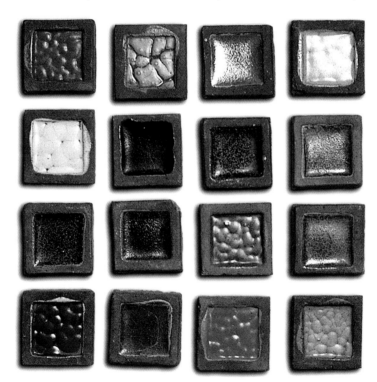

Sometime around 1922 color specialist Ivan Branham was hired. Soon after, patterns that had previously been primarily brown or gray bloomed into greens, oranges, and lavenders. Tile glazes were shown in small color samples such as these for use in showrooms.

terns, reflecting a taste that appears to have been inspired by the pages of the *National Geographic* as well as several scholarly folio volumes on Mayan art that were produced at the turn of the century. By the late 1920s Batchelder was producing Art Deco

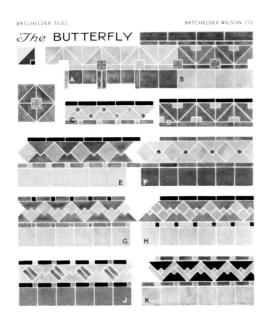

tiles and was responsible for many lavender and black bathrooms. And, although in the early days of his business Batchelder had eschewed high glazes, many of his tiles in the 1920s were glossy.

As the range of patterns expanded, so did the number of places from which Batchelder got his clay. The Alberhill-Corona area in Southern California was his chief continuing source, but in the 1920s the Lincoln Clay Products Company in Placer County also supplied the raw material. Red clay came from Ione, in Amador County, and a small amount of clay originated in Santa Monica.

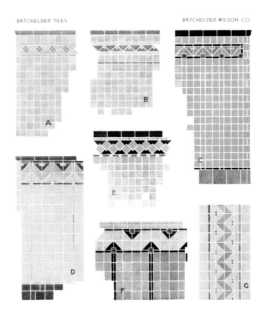

A designer's interest is always aroused in the problem of assembling simple elements into varied patterns. The introduction of a single new shape stimulates the imagination. This particular shape is derived from a four inch diagonal coordinated with our Patina Glaze series. It presents an infinite number of combinations, apparently quite involved, although in fact of the simplest nature. This new unit fits admirably into patterns requiring none other than stock materials.

Colors have been carefully studied in order to offer harmonious combinations with our Patina Glaze Blends. These new colors allow desirable contrasts in almost any scheme which may be selected. They are not "just a few more colors". They have been chosen with definite chromatic values relative to our entire glazed product. They permit the use of two or more contrasting colors in the form of borders and liners with assurance of consistent results.

Batchelder, never stylistically dogmatic, responded to changing popular tastes with a line of Art Deco patterns.

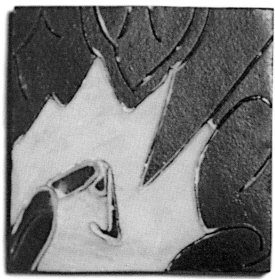

A line of pre-Columbian patterns seemed to have been inspired by the pages of the *National Geographic* as well as several scholarly folio volumes on Mayan art that were produced at the turn of the century.

LAVENDER BLEND

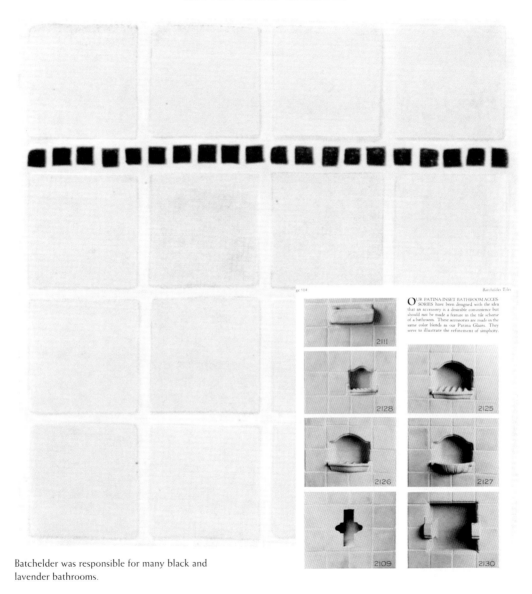

OUR PATINA-INSET BATHROOM ACCES-
SORIES have been designed with the idea
that an accessory is a desirable convenience but
should not be made a feature in the tile scheme
of a bathroom. These accessories are made in the
same color blends as our Patina Glazes. They
serve to illustrate the refinement of simplicity.

Batchelder was responsible for many black and
lavender bathrooms.

A BATHROOM DESIGN OF UNUSUAL INTEREST

❖ BATCHELDER TILES ❖

TILES COMBINE GLAZE, COLOR AND TEXTURE IN SUCH A WAY AS TO MAKE THEM THE LOGICAL CONSTRUCTIVE MATERIAL FOR FOUNTAIN WORK

A garden without a fountain is like a home without a fireplace. Neither one can be justified on purely utilitarian grounds. Each one offers an opportunity for the expression of individual thought and may contribute the final note of beauty to the project.

A 1920s advertisement shows the shift to more colorful tiles, reflecting an Islamic pattern. The installation to the left is the fountain in Batchelder's own backyard. Fountain at right location unknown.

BATCHELDER TILES

SHOWN above is the "Fountain of the Seasons"...typical of the Batchelder originality in design.

A fountain of Batchelder Tiles adds the final touch of distinction to the garden, patio or sun-room. Some have soft, subdued color tones, others sparkle with contrasting glazes.

Many original designs, colors, finishes and glazes for mantels, baths and pavements.

More complete information in the Batchelder "Describe-o-Log." Write for a copy.

BATCHELDER--WILSON COMPANY
2633 Artesian Street, Los Angeles . . . 101 Park Ave., New York City

BATCHELDER TILES

This design (No. 558) illustrates the wide adaptability of Batchelder catalogue materials and shows that a fountain, although essentially beautiful and artistic, is not necessarily expensive.

Is Your Patio or Garden Complete?

SO often an otherwise charming retreat just misses the ideal because it lacks that elusive "something". In most cases a fountain will add the finishing touch of color that gives it *life*.

Perhaps the greatest virtue, and certainly one peculiar to Batchelder Tiles, is that they harmonize with any surroundings...no glaring highlights, no vividly obtrusive colors...only the soft, subdued tones of old tapestries or cheerful glazes that sparkle in harmonious contrasts. The designs are original and essentially artistic.

Your architect or decorator will tell you that Batchelder Tiles offer infinite possibilities for the creation of unique effects in fountains, mantels, baths, pavements or wainscots, because of their great variety of colors, designs, finishes and glazes.

More complete information is embodied in the Batchelder "Describe-o-Log". Write for a copy.

BATCHELDER --- WILSON COMPANY
2634 Artesian Street, Los Angeles · · 101 Park Avenue, New York City

He obtained bentonite, a soft volcanic clay used in underglazing, from a deposit near Amboy in San Bernardino County. At the height of production in the late 1920s, he was using six standard mixtures graded in fired-body colors in a spectrum that ranged from cream to red. According to Waldemar Fenn Dietrich's *The Clay Resources and the Ceramic Industry of California* (1928), Batchelder's workers prepared these mixtures "by jaw crushing, roller-mill grinding, and finally pug-mill mixing and tempering." The batches were then seasoned in moist rooms for at least two weeks before being hand-pressed in plaster molds made at the plant. The tiles were dried in the open air and then in ovens, the total drying process taking about forty-eight hours. They were then ready for the light glaze to be applied and for the final firing.[32]

One of Batchelder's finest installations is the lobby of the Fine Arts Building (1925) on West Seventh Street in downtown Los Angeles. The building was designed by architects Walker and Eisen, one of the largest firms in the city at the time. The building was intended to house artists' studios and to display their wares. Again, lacking business records, it is difficult to say precisely why Batchelder got the job except that by this time his company was capable of producing tiles on a large scale and was well known for its contribution to artistic expression in the manner of the fine arts. Sometimes Batchelder cast very large pieces, such as the huge allegorical lobby sculptures representing artistic disciplines.

The street facade, largely terracotta sheathing by the California-based firm of Gladding, McBean, seems to have been a Beaux-Arts-inflected interpre-

One of Batchelder's
finest installations is the
lobby of the Fine Arts
Building in downtown
Los Angeles, 1925.

Sometimes Batchelder cast very large pieces, such as the huge allegorical sculptures representing the arts that he made for the lobby.

Batchelder supervises the firing of one of the figures.

tation of the facade of the Romanesque cathedral in Lucca, Italy.[33] The interior—more Spanish Renaissance than any other style—contrasted with this updated medievalism. The arcaded two-story main lobby consisted entirely of Batchelder tile, much of it common stock but also some new details designed especially for the building. The large female figures representing the arts were certainly unusual and must have been difficult to conceive and execute.

The interior of Our Lady of Victory Chapel at the St. Catherine's College in St. Paul, Minnesota (1923) was an even larger work. The chapel, designed by H. A. Sullwold, was Batchelder's largest commission. He was probably chosen for this project because of his earlier connections with the

200·204

Minneapolis Guild of Handicraft just across the Mississippi River from St. Paul. The interior is almost entirely Batchelder tile including the Stations of the Cross. Unfortunately the beautiful hanging lamps that were a part of the original composition have been removed.

The chapel's interior is entirely Batchelder including the Stations of the Cross.

The Chapel at St. Catherine's
College in St Paul Minnesota was
Batchelder's largest commission.

Local entrepreneur J. W. Hobbs was inspired by New York's Chrysler Building to try to achieve the same effect for Vancouver. He believed that this natural port should consolidate its business activities in a building that would celebrate the city's association with the sea.

We know much more about the Marine Building (1929-30) in Vancouver, thanks to a janitor's chance discovery of letter when cleaning out an old desk. It begins: "If anyone knows the story of the Marine Building, it's me. I've seen everything...." The story that unfolds concerns the ambition of a local entrepreneur, J. W. Hobbs, who was inspired by New York's Chrysler Building to try to achieve the same effect for Vancouver. He believed that this natural port should consolidate its business activities in a building that would celebrate the city's association with the sea and would reflect a progressive style, in this case Art Deco. The architects, McCarter and Nairne of Vancouver, followed Hobb's interest in the nautical by commissioning sculpture of famous Canadian ships and seamen as the decoration of the exterior. The same theme is carried out in the interior, but it is curiously mixed with ornament, all in Batchelder tiles, derived from Mayan architecture. No one seems to know the reason for this decidedly un-Canadian venture or for the fact that an effigy of a ship on the north wall next to the main lobby directory is upside down. And as the anonymous writer noted, "rumour has it there is a ghost on 'D' level. I won't dispute that... but just try and find me."

Marine Building, Vancouver, British Columbia today, left, and as it appeared in the 1920s, above.

Batchelder Tiles had showrooms in several major US cities including these in Oakland (above) and Chicago (below).

The 1920s marked the high point in the history of Batchelder's tile business. The tiles were now advertised and used throughout the United States and Canada. Batchelder was proud of the firm's showrooms in major U.S. cities, especially of the one at 101 Park Avenue in New York. Business was going so well that he could afford to splurge on a new guest house and garage at his home on the Arroyo Seco.

In the 1920s Batchelder added a new guesthouse and garage
to his home on the Arroyo Seco.

ATHENS OF THE WEST

1925—1957

Ever since his experience at the Central School of Arts and Crafts at Birmingham, where the school was literally across the street from "a large and very complete Museum of Fine and Industrial Arts," the idea of a similar museum in Pasadena had been one of Batchelder's principal preoccupations.[1] The formation of a Music and Art Association in 1911 had renewed that interest, and money was raised for a museum on the campus of Throop Polytechnic Institute. The art galleries did not materialize there, but Ernest pursued his dream of a museum where painting and sculpture could be exhibited and where there might be an allied school that encouraged the arts.

In 1922 he wrote a long article for the *Pasadena Star-News* advocating the creation of such a facility, to be called the Pasadena Art Institute. The article was written, Batchelder said, in connection with an exhibition at Caltech of some forty paintings by California artists. He thought the show was "important because it is representative of the work that is being done here and is clearly an indication of the fact that we have long neglected one of our best assets." An art museum would help to encourage established local artists and might attract others who would make Pasadena "the Athens of the West."[2] Noting that it was "a city beautiful in its homes, its gardens, its streets through our initiative as individuals," he went on to assert what was to become a deeply held conviction of many Pasadenans: "We seem agreed that we do not hope for tanneries, steel mills or cotton mills to find location here." Recalling his Arts and Crafts bias, he applied it to the Pasadena situation and suggested that light industries be established that would bring "employment to highly skilled designers and artisans, the production of fine jewelry, the printing and binding of beautiful books, the designing and weaving of tapestries, gold and silver smithing, carving, mural painting." A museum would display these local wares and also local collections of foreign works, such as A.C. Vroman's "remarkable collection of Japanese netsukis [sic]." Because there was no Pasadena museum to house his holdings of netsukes, Vroman, an outstanding photographer, bibliophile, and collector, had given them to the Metropolitan Museum of Art in New York.[3]

As to the associated school, it would, Batchelder proposed, be something like the Rhode Island School of Design, financed largely by industries within the community. He pointed out that Pasadena already had such an institution, thanks to the donations of Susan G. Stickney. The presence of the successful Stickney Memorial School of Art, an annex of the Music and Art Association, indicated, he thought, that such an enterprise was possible.[4]

It may be that in this effort Batchelder, a recognized writer on the arts, was acting as a conduit for the convictions of his friend, the astronomer and cultural leader George Ellery Hale. A native of Chicago, Hale had been sent to Pasadena by the Carnegie Foundation in 1903 to open an observatory on Mount Wilson. He stayed on to become a trustee of the Throop Polytechnic Institute, which he was chiefly responsible for converting from a trade school with liberal-arts overtones into a scientific institution. It was he who brought the Nobel laureate physicist Robert Millikan to Throop in 1920 and saw to it that Millikan became the president of the new institution that grew out of Throop: the California Institute of Technology (Caltech), modeled on Hale's beloved alma mater, the Massachusetts Institute of Technology. Even the term that Batchelder had used to describe Pasadena—"the Athens of the West"—originated with Hale. Similarly, "the Pasadena Art Institute," a designation Batchelder had invoked to describe the imagined museum, was an echo of the Art Institute of Chicago which had been Hale's haunt when he was young. Indeed, just before submitting his 1922 article to the *Star-News*, Batchelder gave Hale a draft and asked for his corrections and additions.[5]

Hale's specialty in education might have been technical training, but his cultural interests were extraordinarily broad. As administrator of the Mount Wilson Observatory, he had commissioned his old friend and fellow Chicagoan Daniel Burnham to design it; it was to be Burnham's last work, completed after his death. With the example of that outstanding architect and city planner in mind, he persuaded the Throop authorities to employ Myron Hunt, another Chicagoan, and Elmer Grey, also a native of the Midwest, to plan the campus and design a major building for it. However, when he discovered at the Panama-California Exposition in San Diego in 1915 that Bertram Goodhue, one of America's finest architects (and his personal favorite) was available, he engaged him to continue with an even more ambitious plan.

In 1926 Hale and Batchelder launched a fund-raising campaign for a new building with a tiled dome on the site of an old house in Carmelita Park, just above Colorado Boulevard near the Arroyo Seco.[6] Before his death in 1924, Bertram Goodhue had recommended Clarence W. Stein, a New York architect who worked in the Goodhue style, to carry on. In March 1927 the *Star-News* carried a long description of the proposed edifice, which would consist of a main exhibition hall and forty-five smaller galleries.[7] One non-journalistic observer estimated that this structure, equipped with the latest ideas in lighting, would cost about $1,500,000.[8] Arthur H. Fleming, a local philanthropist who had funded many projects at Caltech, gushed that the planned complex would "vie with the Taj Mahal, Agra, India in its beauty."[9] The following week, he found himself obliged to write a letter to the paper denying that he would be the donor.[10]

Disappointment followed, but it did not immediately cool the ardor of Hale and Batchelder for the project. Batchelder's commitment was undoubtedly strengthened by the immutable determination of his wife to bring chamber music to Pasadena. In spite of the fact that the city had never had any experience with this esoteric form, Alice founded her Coleman Concerts in 1904 and converted a reluctant audience to enthusiasm for the performances in which she often participated. Her hours on the telephone attracted musicians and, finally, well-off patrons so that by the 1920s, her concerts had become a solid Pasadena tradition.

In fact, Alice was intimately involved with her husband's and Hale's ideas perhaps with an ultimate goal of building a performance venue for the Coleman Concerts. As a trustee of the museum and with fund-raising knowledge, she was an asset to the institution. Unfortunately, Alice's efforts were not

enough to see the museum built. In order to buy the park the trustees had secured a mortgage which had to be cleared. The Music and Art Association, of which she and Ernest were founding members, sold its Stickney Memorial School property to raise money for the cause. A spokesman explained that the idea was to raise money for the construction of the museum rather than to clear the mortgage but the situation did not improve.[11]

One of several preliminary drawings made in 1927 by Clarence Stein for the Pasadena Art Institute.

Facing this bleak situation, Batchelder turned his attention back to the Caltech campus. He wrote to Hale in 1931 after the Depression had crippled the economy, asking if a site and funds could be found there. Hale's reply was discouraging: "The only hope would seem to be in some miraculous donor, sufficiently interested to provide the funds. But where can such a donor be found?"[12] Batchelder subsequently refocused on the Carmelita Park site. As late as 1935 he was still urging development of a museum there. In February of that year, he invited his friend Hale to a dinner at the University Club, where directors of the Pasadena Community Playhouse Association, the Music and Art Association, the Coleman Chamber Music Association and the Pasadena Art Institute would meet "to explore the possibilities for a closer coordination of these groups in relation to the development of Carmelita as a cultural center."[13] There the matter stood until after World War II. Finally in the 1950s, a differently constituted Pasadena Museum of Art opened in the 1924 Chinese-style mansion of Grace Nicholson, a dealer in Asian art, which had been bequeathed to the city.

Years earlier, Batchelder had completely given up any thought of returning to the East. Even business adversity could not daunt him in his pursuit of high culture for Pasadena. Many factors contributed to his growing commitment, chief among them being the recognition he was receiving as a civic leader—most notably as an articulate spokesman for worthy causes. For example, when local women's clubs asked him to encourage tree planting along Colorado Boulevard, the core of Pasadena's central business district, Batchelder readily complied, in the process coming up with the slogan "Trees for Business." Writing in the *Star-News*, he pointed out that "judiciously planted trees are recognized as an intimate part of an architectural unity." He particularly championed the use of the *Cocos plumosa* palm that few cities outside Southern California could hope to grow.[14]

In asking Batchelder to further their cause, the women's clubs were acknowledging his leadership in Pasadena's manifestation of the nationwide City Beautiful movement, a movement his comrade George Ellery Hale also avidly supported. Batchelder's interest in city planning made him an obvious choice for appointment in 1923 to the Pasadena Planning Commission on which Hale already served. This was an interesting time in the city's history. In the 1900 U.S. census, taken just a year before Batchelder arrived in Pasadena, the population of the growing country town, which had been founded in 1874 as the Indiana Colony, was estimated at 9,117. By 1920 it had risen to 45,354, and ten years later it would reach 75,086.[15] Known as the richest city in per capita income in the nation, it obviously needed public buildings to reflect its growing importance.

In July 1929, after the completion of the facelifting of all the buildings on Colorado Boulevard, the *Star-News* printed an article by Batchelder praising their "individuality of style."[16] He had had little to do with the Art Deco and Spanish Colonial Revival facades that had been attached to the predominantly Victorian buildings, but he was deeply involved with the plan that was developed for Pasadena's

Civic Center, which included the building of an art museum at the west end of its main axis on Holly Street.[17] He served on the jury that selected the architects of the new library, auditorium, and city hall that were to be the anchors of the beautiful Beaux-Arts cross-axial plan. He and his fellow jurists—Hale, the Los Angeles architects Robert Farquhar and Pierpont Davis, and the chairman of the Pasadena Planning Commission, Stuart French—decided that participation in the competi-tion for the design of major buildings should be lim-ited to California architects. Eventually, they select-ed the firm of Bakewell and Brown, architects of the San Francisco City Hall, to design its Pasadena counterpart. The initial proposal called for a gigan-tic Mission Revival entrance, an enlarged version of the campanario at Mission San Gabriel. But the jury wisely chose the rendering of a more moderate facade that combined aspects of the Spain's Escorial with the domes of the Invalides in Paris and the

Batchelder served on the jury that selected the architects of the new library, auditorium, and city hall that were to be the anchors of the beautiful Beaux-Arts cross-axial plan. Bakewell and Brown, architects of the San Francisco City Hall, designed Pasadena's counterpart (left).

In 1924, Elmer Grey designed the Pasadena Playhouse (above) The interior is the work of Alson Clark, a painter, and Charles Gibbs Adams, a landscape architect.

Pasadena Public Library, Myron Hunt architect (right).

New Cathedral in Salamanca. The Pasadena firm of Bennett and Haskell was chosen to do the civic auditorium in a style reminiscent of the Italian Renaissance; Edwin Bergstrom of Los Angeles was the principal designer. The Pasadena-based Myron Hunt planned the mainly Spanish Renaissance public library of which Batchelder was to write prophetically (and correctly), "The library is a building we shall love the more the longer we live with it."[18]

As Batchelder became more involved with civic causes, he delegated business matters to others. Although amazingly productive in the 1920s, Batchelder's company, like many other tile-making firms at the time, went under in the Great Depression. Tile installations were not, after all, essential to buildings, and the steep decline in construction that occurred after the stock market crash in October 1929 dramatically reduced the general

The *Pasadena Star-News* reported that the demand for Manker's slipcast ware had exceeded his capacity to produce it.

demand for tiles. Within a couple of years Batchelder's factory was sold to pay outstanding debts. As Alan Batchelder recalled, "In 1931 my parents were paying my bills at Pomona College; in 1932 I was working my way through college." From 1932 until 1936, Ernest was unemployed. For a few years, Alice's income from piano lessons was literally the only income the family had.

As the national economy slowly began recovering in the mid-1930s, however, Batchelder's interest in the production of ceramics was rekindled. William Manker, formerly employed in the design department of Batchelder's factory, had been experimenting with slipcast ware. Apparently, Batchelder and Manker agreed to a partnership that would put

this work into production. The *Pasadena Star-News,* covering an exhibition of Manker's ceramics in Caltech's Dabney Lounge, converted temporarily to a gallery, noted that "the demand for the ware has exceeded the capacity to produce it." The Caltech show, the reporter advised, was a "preview" of what Manker and Batchelder would do with a "refined industry," in which the two principals would avoid "what is generally referred to as 'mass production.'" Its trademark would be its "restrained simplicity."[19]

Evidently Manker never really worked with Batchelder, although the site of Manker's "small kiln built at the eastern city limits," referred to by the newspaper, was undoubtedly the place in Titleyville, an unincorporated area on the east side of Pasadena, where Batchelder eventually located his new small-scale operation on Kinneloa Avenue. The ware he made there was similar in style to the bowls, vases, and platters that Manker, a founder of the pottery section of the art department of Scripps College in Claremont, was producing in the late 1930s.[20]

In 1936, employing only four or five workers, Batchelder opened his little shop and began producing slipcast pieces suitable for flower arrangements. He obtained clay from California, Tennessee, Nevada, Georgia, and even England.[21] Alan Batchelder, who worked there for a short time, described the production process this way: "The individual pieces would be delicate to the feel—semi-porcelain in quality—and glazed in gently graded colors favoring pastel shades...[They] would be cast from slips in plaster-of-paris molds, then dried, hand-finished to remove mold lines and other imperfections, and finally, fired to bisque, glazed and re-fired."

Batchelder spraying glaze over a slipcast piece.

In 1936, employing only four or five workers, Batchelder opened a little shop and began producing slipcast pieces.

Alan recalled that Ivan Branham, the color specialist who had worked for Batchelder in the 1920s, advised him on the chemistry involved in this experiment. Ernest recognized his assistance by giving him thirteen shares in the new business. Alan remembered that Branham's death in 1937 was a "grievous blow" to his father; he had been "a close friend who stood ready to give one advice and assistance on technical matters in a complex field of chemistry as well as friendly counsel."[22] Batchelder employed people living in the neighborhood, mainly Mexican-Americans, to assist him in the process. He deeply appreciated the hard work and care they contributed to the products known as Batchelder

Ceramics or, sometimes, Kinneloa Pottery and inscribed on the underside either Pasadena or Kinneloa, followed by the number of the design.

After Alice's death in June, 1948, Ernest decided to retire. In August, 1949 he sold the business (including its name) to James Stuart Bruce who did not continue the production of ceramics. Old age and a bout with lead poisoning discouraged and exhausted Batchelder. He moved from the main house into the guest house he had built next to his garage during the 1920s. In 1951 he retired from the presidency of the Pasadena Community Playhouse Association but maintained his membership on the advisory board of Pasadena Public Library, whose architecture he so admired.

On August 6, 1957, Ernest Allen Batchelder succumbed to arteriosclerosis at the Huntington Memorial Hospital in Pasadena, thus ending fifty-six years of enthusiastic service to his beloved city of Pasadena and to the fine arts.

CHRONOLOGY

Ernest A. Batchelder (1876?–1957)

1876 (or 1875) Ernest Allen Batchelder born in Francestown?, New Hampshire.

1895 Graduates from Massachusetts Normal Art Institute, Boston.

1901 Assists Professor Denman W. Ross at the Harvard Summer School of Design. Moves to Pasadena, California, where he is employed by the Throop Polytechnic Institute.

1904 Assists Frederick Alan Whiting in assembling Southwestern Arts and Crafts for Louisiana Purchase International Exposition, St. Louis.

1905-06 Tours Europe and studies in England.

1905-09 Teaches design at the Minneapolis Handicraft Guild Summer School.

1908 Publishes *The Principles of Design*. Takes another trip to England and the Continent.

1909 Resigns from Throop and buys property on Arroyo Seco. Builds a house.

1910 Builds shop behind house. Begins to design and craft tile there. Publishes *Design in Theory and Practice*.

1912 Moves tile business to a larger shop at 769 Broadway (now Arroyo Parkway). Marries Alice Coleman.

1914 Commissioned to design and decorate the interior of the Dutch Chocolate Shop in downtown Los Angeles. A son, Alan Coleman Batchelder, is born.

1920 Moves his tile company from Pasadena to larger quarters in Los Angeles.

1932 His business fails in the Depression.

1936 Begins making slip-cast ware.

1948 Alice dies.

1949 Ernest sells business and retires.

1957 Dies August 6 in Pasadena.

ACKNOWLEDGMENTS

Lynn Dumenil, David Gebhard, Joseph Taylor, Phyllis Hudson, and Sue Schechter read early drafts of this book. Phil Freshman edited a late one. I am deeply indebted to these friends for their advice but hasten to add that they are responsible only for the good parts.

As every author knows, a book depends upon contributions from many sources. I especially thank the members of the Batchelder family, particularly Ernest's son, Alan, who talked to me many times about his father. His reminiscences and his answers to many telephoned questions form the point of view of my story. He also lent me family pictures and a great many vintage photographs of his father's production of tiles. I will never forget Alan and forever will be sad that he did not live to see the finished product. He did read an early draft and gave it careful criticism.

Others who have helped me are Albert Anderson, Marcia G. Anderson, Bea Batchelder, E. Alan Batchelder, John Brinkman, Norman Cohen, Theodore Coleman, Fauntleroy Compton, Alan Crawford, Patty Dean, Caroline Garner, Kathleen Harnett, Blain Hightower, Pamela D. Kingsbury, Donna A. McQuade, Elva Meline, Shiela Menzies, Megs Meriwether, Richard Mohr, Tom Owen, Miv Schaaf, Marie Tapp and Susan Tunick.

I have already noted my dependence on the Batchelder family archives for vintage black-and-white photographs. Among the most important photographers represented in this collection are the Mott Studios in Los Angeles and the Martin Studios in Pasadena. I also am grateful to people who lent me their early photographs or shared their more recent takes with me. These are Peter Shamray, Pam Homes, Jim Lewis, Marjolyn McDougall, Karen Melvin, Ken Miedema, John Miller and Richard Mouck, Gibbs Smith, Alexander Vertikoff and James and Pierette Winter.

It is a pleasure once again to thank my friend Kurt Hauser who, with the help of his wife Grace, made this what I believe is a beautiful book. I do not type and certainly do not use a word processor, so I am especially grateful to Jean Viggiano who does.

Finally thanks to Ann Gray, a publisher and editor who not only saw the good in this book but also managed its publication with a sensitivity that is beloved by authors.

ILLUSTRATION CREDITS

All images are from the collection of the author and taken by him or by an unknown photographer unless noted otherwise.

Alex Vertikoff photographer: 7, 35-37, 39, 53, 58, 62, 63, 74, 80, 81, 83, 85-90, 93.

Peter Shamray photographer: cover, title page, 8, 11, 12, 16, 17, 34b, 40, 47r, 48t, 49t, 50, 51, 54, 55, 56, 57t, 70, 72, 73, 75, 94, 95, 97, 103r, 104, 105.

13, 15, Photographer unknown. From the collection of Dr. Robert Winter.

19b, Courtesy of the Archives, California Institute of Technology.

21, 34t, 69, Photographer unknown. From the collection of Dr. Robert Winter.

23, Karen Melvin photographer.

31, E. Alan Batchelder photographer.

44, 63, 106, 107, Collection of Batchelder family.

64, 65, Frederick Martin photographer. Courtesy Jim Lewis.

66, John Martin and Richard Mouck photographers.

33, 67t, Collection of Dr. Robert Winter.

68l, Courtesy Pam Homes.

14, 19t, 24, 25, 26, 30, 32, 41-43, 45-47l, 48b, 52t, 57b, 59, 58bl, 61, 68r, 71, 78l, 79, 100, From the collection of Dr. Robert Winter.

60bl, Gibbs Smith photographer. Collection of Dr. Robert Winter.

78r, Photographer unknown. Courtesy Jim Lewis.

58, 67b Frederick Martin photographer. Collection of Batchelder family.

60rt, rb, Courtesy Pamela D. Kingsbury. Henry Nelson, Nelson & Nelson Creative Photography.

60tl, Swan Studio Photographers. Collection of Batchelder family.

76, 1929 Batchelder Tile Catalog of Patina Glazes. Collection of Batchelder family.

34t, 52b, 69, 77, Photographers unknown. Collection of Batchelder family.

82r, Mott Studios photographers. Collection of Dr. Robert Winter.

82l, Mott Studios photographers. Collection of Batchelder family.

84l, Northwestern Photographic Studio, Inc. Photographer. Collection of Batchelder family.

91, Dominion Photo Co., Collection of Batchelder family.

92t, Pictorial Publicity Studio photographers, Collection of Batchelder family.

92b, Hedrich-Blessing Studio photographers, Collection of Batchelder family.

98, Artist unknown. Collection of Ann Scheid.

101, From "Myron Hunt: The Search for a Regional Architecture," Baxter Art Gallery. (1984 Hennessey & Ingalls) Courtesy California Institute of Technology.

102, Tim Andersen Photographer. Collection of Dr. Robert Winter.

103l, J. Allen Hawkins photographer. Collection of Batchelder family.

NOTES

CHAPTER ONE

1. An article, "Ernest Batchelder: Exponent of the Practical in Art," in the *Pasadena Star*, of November 15, 1915, also supports the 1876 date. Most of the information in this paragraph comes from a letter Alan Batchelder sent to me, dated August 4, 1988. See also, Frederick Clifton Pierce, Batchelder, Batcheller Genealogy (Chicago, 1898).

2. *The Batchelder Family News-Journal* 4 (April 1974), unpaginated.

3. Edward C. Kirkland, *A History of American Economic Life* (New York: Appleton-Century-Crofts, 1951), 398.

4. See Ernest Batchelder, *The Principles of Design* (Chicago: Inland Printer Company, 1908), Preface, in which he specifically credits Ross for the philosophy of design he used.

5. See Janet Ferrari, "Throop University" in Timothy J. Andersen, Eudorah M. Moore, and Robert W. Winter, eds., *California Design, 1910.* Exh. Cat. (1974; reprint, Salt Lake City: Peregrine Smith, 1989), 60.

6. James. A. B. Scherer, "The Throop Idea," *Arroyo Craftsman* 1 (October 1909), unpaginated.

7. A fine description of the little-recognized exhibition of American arts and crafts at the St. Louis fair is found in Beverly K. Brandt, "Worthy and Carefully Selected," *Archives of American Art Journal* 28, no. 1 (1988): 2-16.

8. Batchelder to Whiting, April 1, 1904. *Archives of American Art* (hereafter AAA) microfilm roll 1747, frame 286. I am deeply indebted to James Elliott Benjamin for sharing with me his discovery of the Batchelder-Whiting correspondence.

9. Whiting to Denman W. Ross, telegram, April 8, 1904, AAA microfilm roll 1747, frame 292.

10. Ross to Whiting, telegram, April 8, 1904, AAA microfilm roll 1747, frame 291.

11. Whiting to Batchelder, telegram, April 11, 1904, AAA microfilm roll 1747, frame 293.

12. Whiting to Batchelder, April 11, 1904, AAA microfilm roll 1747, frames 296 and 297.

13. Batchelder to Whiting, April 26, 1904, AAA microfilm roll 1747, frame 305.

14. Batchelder to Whiting, May 16, 1904, AAA microfilm roll 1748, frame 7.

15. Batchelder to Whiting, April 30, 1904, AAA microfilm roll 1747, frame 310.

16. Batchelder to Whiting, April 26, 1904, AAA microfilm roll 1747, frame 303.

17. Batchelder to Whiting, May 6, 1904, AAA microfilm roll 1748, frame 9.

18. Ibid., frame 10.

19. Batchelder to Whiting, May 13, 1904, AAA microfilm roll 1748, frame 9.

20. Batchelder to Whiting, April 26, 1904, AAA microfilm roll 1747, frame 304.

21. Batchelder to Whiting, May 6, 1904. AAA microfilm roll 1748, frame 8.

22. Ibid., frame 10.

23. *The Craftsman* 8 (May 1905): 267. See Marcia G. Anderson, "Art for Life's Sake: The Handicraft Guild of Minneapolis" in Michael Conforti, ed. *Art and Life on the Mississippi, 1890-1915* (Newark: University of Delaware Press, 1994), 131.

24. See Darrell Garwood, *Artist in Iowa: A Life of Grant Wood* (New York: W.W. Norton & Company, 1944) especially pp. 29-33.

25. One of Batchelder's letters is headed "The Principles of Design: A Course in Design by Correspondence." Batchelder to Frederick Allen Whiting, April 30, 1904. Archives of American Art, Smithsonian Institution, Washington, D.C. microfilm roll 1747, frame 309.
Garwood has Wood graduating from high school and immediately going to Minneapolis in the summer of 1910 to study with his idol, Batchelder. In truth, Batchelder had retired from Minneapolis and was running his own school in his backyard in Pasadena that summer. Garwood's version probably rests on interviews with Wood, who was enthusiastic but whose memory may not have been clear. It is possible, however, that Wood attended one of the sessions Batchelder led between 1905 and 1909.

26. Batchelder to Whiting, June 29, [1905]. AAA microfilm roll 300, frame 425.

27. Ibid., frame 426.

28. Batchelder to Whiting, December 3, 1904, AAA microfilm roll 300, frame 443. He was, of course, referring to the work of the master craftsman Henry Chapman Mercer of the Moravian Pottery and Tile Works in Doylestown, Pennsylvania, and Hugh C. Robertson of the Dedham Pottery in Dedham, Massachusetts.

29. Alan Batchelder noted that "stunning" was the word his father often used "to connote praise of the highest degree." Letter to me, August 8, 1989.

30. Batchelder to Whiting, February 17, 1905, AAA microfilm roll 300, frame 457. The letterhead under which he wrote was that of the Pacific Manual Training Teachers Association, with Batchelder listed as president; Miss A. McMahon, Redlands, vice president; Miss Ella

V. Dobbs, Pasadena, secretary; and Miss Ada Blanchard, Los Angeles, treasurer.

31. Batchelder to Whiting, November 15, 1905, AAA microfilm roll 300, frame 478. Batchelder was writing from his room at Chipping-Campden's Noel Arms Hotel , "as fine as anything Dickens ever dug up."

32. The most complete account of the Chipping-Campden experiment is in Alan Crawford, *C.R. Ashbee: Architect, Designer, Romantic Socialist* (New Haven and London: Yale University Press, 1985), 100-48, 153-62.

33. For Janet's amusing and discerning description of this visit, see Robert W. Winter, "American Sheaves from 'C.R.A.' and Janet Ashbee, *Journal of the Society of Architectural Historians* 30 (December 1971): 318-20.

34. Ashbee to Whiting, April 8, 1903,AAA microfilm roll 300, frames 369-70.

35. Batchelder to Whiting, November 15, 1905, AAA microfilm roll 300, frame 478.

36. Ibid.

37. Ernest Batchelder, "Why the Handicraft Guild at Chipping-Campden Has Not Been a Business Success," *The Craftsman* 15 (November 1908): 175.

38. Information given to me by Alan Crawford in a letter dated January 21, 1978.

39. Ernest Batchelder, "The World's Advance in Industrial Education," *The Craftsman* 15 (November 1908): 175.

40. He is probably referring to his father.

41. Batchelder to Whiting, May 21, 1907, AAA microfilm roll 300, frame 495.

42. Ibid., frames 496-97.

43. *Pasadena Daily News*, August 26, 1908.

44. Ibid.

45. This series of Batchelder articles in The Craftsman included: "The Abiding Lesson of Gothic Architecture," 15 (February 1909): 533-48; "The Medieval Craftsman" 15 (March 1909): 681-90; "How Medieval Craftsmen Created Beauty by Meeting the Constructive Problems of Gothic Architecture," 16 (April 1909) : 44-49; "Carving...Its Purpose in Architecture," 16 (April 1909): 60-69; "Tool-Wrought Ornament of the Medieval Blacksmith," 16 (May 1909): 148-59.

46. *Pasadena Daily News*, May 23, 1909.

47. Ibid.

48. *Pasadena Daily News*, June 3, 1909..

49. Ibid.

50. See also "The Arroyo Guild: An Organization of Craftsmen," *Southwest Contractor and Manufacturer* 4 (January 15, 1910): 14.

51. The permit was for a "6 rm 1st fr. bung." and was dated September 8, 1909. According to the permt the cost of the house would be $2,600. Records of the Pasadena Planning Department, Pasadena City Hall.

52. Batchelder used a sketch of the facade of the house in an advertisement for his "School of Design and Handicraft" in the *Pasadena Daily News*, September 16, 1909. The sleeping porch was conspicuous in the picture. Evidently, his scheme had expanded after the permit was issued eight days earlier.

53. For more on Easton and his work in the neighborhood, see Tim Andersen, "Louis B. Easton" in Robert Winter, ed., *Toward a Simpler Way of Life: The Arts and Crafts Architects of California* (Berkeley, Los Angeles, London: University of California Press, 1997), 149-58.

54. *Pasadena Daily News*, February 19, 1910.

55. *Pasadena Evening Star*, February 5, 1910.

56. Records of the Pasadena Planning Department, Pasadena City Hall.

CHAPTER TWO

1. Ernest Batchelder, *The Principles of Design* (Chicago: Inland Printer Company, 1908), Preface.

2. James M. Dennis, *Renegade Regionalists: The Modern Independence of Grant Wood*, Thomas Hart Benton and John Steuart Curry (Madison: University if Wisconsin Press, 1998), 178-182. *Dow's Composition*, originally published in 1899 went through several editions, the last in 1941.

3. Ernest Batchelder, *Design in Theory and Practice* (New York: The Macmillan Company, 1910), 141-69.

4. *International Studio* 22 (June 1908): ccxvii.

5. *International Studio* 42 (December 1910): unpaginated.

6. *The Outlook* 96 (December 1910): 792.

7. *American Library Association Booklist* 7 (November 1910): 95.

8. *Encyclopedia Britannica*, 11th ed., s.v., "Tiles". See also, *The Decorative Tile in Architecture and Interiors* by Tony Herbert and Kathryn Huggins, an interpretive essay on 19th century tile in England and Europe with spectacular photography of historic installations (Phaidon Press Ltd., London, 1995). See also, *Tiles: 1000 Years of Architectural Decoration* by Hans van Lemmen (Harry Abrams, New York, 1993).

9. See Bert Randall Denker and Ellen Paul Denker, "Low Art Tiles Works" in Wendy Kaplan,et al, "The Art that is Life." The Arts and Crafts Movement in America, 1875-1920. (Boston: Little Brown and Company, 1987), 69.

10. See Elizabeth Aslin, *The Aesthetic Movement* (New York and Washington: Frederick A. Praeger, 1969), especially 128-44. See also, *American Art Tile 1876-1941* by Norman Karlson (Rizzoli, 1998).

11. Some years later E. B. MacLaughlin, a reporter for the *Pasadena Star-News* summarized an interview with Batchelder as follows: "Greatest of American potters, according to Mr. Batchelder, is the famous Mercer of Doylestown, Pa. The Pasadenan admits with pride that he is a Mercer disciple. Mercer, he said, was "300 years out of his time," probably the only modern artist retaining the glorious touch of the Medieval masters. . . .When the potter of Pasadena makes a vase, he knows it is one that the master, Mercer, might approve." *Pasadena Star-News*, April 11, 1948.

12. Batchelder, *Principles*, 96-97.

13. See Joseph A. Taylor, "Creating Beauty from the Earth: The Tiles of California," in Kenneth R. Trapp, ed., *The Arts and Crafts Movement in California: Living the Good Life* (New York, London, Paris: Abbeville Press, 1993), especially 111-13.

14. Ernest Batchelder, "A Little History of Batchelder Tiles," 1925-26, unpaginated. Copy in collection of the author. Batchelder's estimate is incorrect if he meant that 1913 was the year he began making tiles.

15. Batchelder, "Little History."

16. Pasadena City Building Permit No. 9369, October 1911. In the permit, it was called the "Batchelder Craft Shop" and originally must have been an exhibition space that later was adapted to factory use. Permits dated December 8, 1912, and November 7, 1916, indicate further expansion. The address was 769 South Broadway (now South Arroyo Parkway). Nothing remains of this building.
17. Joseph Taylor, letter to the author, October 3, 1989.
18. The quote is from a tiny, unpaginated booklet, "Batchelder Tiles Made in Pasadena, Batchelder and Brown," published under the imprint of "Ye Colonial Art Shop, Pasadena." Since his partner Frederick L. Brown was associated with Batchelder in 1916, as evidenced in Pasadena City Building Permit No. 6570, February 10, 1916, I assume the pamphlet was published around that time. So far as I know, the only remaining copy of this booklet is in the Alan Batchelder collection.
19. Ibid.
20. See Robert C. Twombly, *Frank Lloyd Wright: His Life and His Architecture* (New York: John Wiley and Sons, 1979), 81-90.
21. Alan's recollection was that his father burned all of Alice's personal correspondence a few days after her death in 1948.
22. Ernest took out a permit on May 8, 1912. It was marked only "alt. to res., $250." Pasadena City Building Permit book, permit no. missing.
23. This information was given to me in a conversation with Anne's sister, Kathleen Harnett, of Long Beach, California, in 1975. According to a newspaper story written thirty five years after the Dutch Chocolate Shop commission, Batchelder and Harnett had only five days to make the designs and provide samples before they were awarded the $65,000 contract. *Pasadena Star-News*, April 11, 1948.
24. As quoted in Peter B. Wight, "The Chocolate Shop," *Western Architect* (September 1924): 105. Wight wrote that Batchelder had made sketches for these panels when he was in Holland and Belgium but that the figures of boys and girls in the foreground were added later. Perhaps this is where the Harnetts were involved. I tend to believe that Anne Harnett was the principal artist. This was the opinion expressed in 1974 to me in a conversation with Fauntleroy Compton, another worker in Batchelder's factory.
25. Batchelder, "Little History."
26. Ibid.
27. Ibid.
28. See, for example, William Morris, *News from Nowhere* (1891; reprint, London and Boston: Routledge and Kegan Paul, 1970), 82.
29. Ernest Batchelder, "The Arts and Crafts Movement in America: Work or Play" *The Craftsman* 16 (August 1909), 548.
30. This information was given to me in a conversation with Fauntleroy Compton in 1974. Batchelder certainly was aware that he strayed from the true path according to Morris. In the late 1930s, after having lost his tile business in the depths of the Great Depression, he opened a workshop that produced a relatively small number of ceramic products. In 1948 he told a reporter that he liked the shop better than the factory: "I don't want to expand," he said. "I've been there before." *Pasadena Star-News*, April 11, 1948.
31. See Mary Davis Mac Naughton, *Art at Scripps: The Early Years* exh. Cat. (Claremont, Calif.: Galleries of the Claremont Colleges, 1988), 16.
32. Dietrich, *The Clay Resources and the Ceramic Industry of California.* Bulletin No. 99 (Sacramento: California State Printing Office, 1928), 97-98.
33. See Donald J. Schippers, "Walker and Eisen: Twenty Years of Los Angeles Architecture, 1920-1940," *Southern California Quarterly* 46 (December 1964), 371-94.

CHAPTER THREE
1. Ernest Batchelder, "The World's Advance in Industrial Education," *The Craftsman* 15 (November 1908): 40.
2. Ernest Batchelder, "Art Museum and School Vital Need of Pasadena," *Pasadena Star-News*, April 1, 1922.
3. Ibid.
4. Ibid.
5. Batchelder to George Ellery Hale, March 23, 1922. Hale Papers, California Institute of Technology, Pasadena, Archives, Box 11: "City Planning Committee."
6. Arthur H. Fleming to Clarence S. Stein, April 8, 1926. Hale Papers, Caltech Archives, Box 72: "Pasadena Art Institute."
7. *Pasadena Star-News*, March 31, 1927.
8. Frederick Allen Whiting to Lawrence T. Coleman, March 24, 1926. Hale Papers, Caltech Archives, Box 72: "Pasadena Art Institute." This is the same Whiting whom we encountered in connection with the Louisiana Purchase International Exposition of 1904. In 1926 he was director of the Cleveland Museum of Art.
9. *Pasadena Star-News*, March 31, 1927.
10. *Pasadena Star-News*, April 8, 1927.
11. *Pasadena Star-News*, September 8, 1932, and April 6, 1934.
12. Hale to Batchelder, April 21, 1931. Hale Papers, Caltech Archives, Box 72: "Pasadena Art Institute."
13. Batchelder to Hale, February 5, 1935. Hale Papers, Caltech Archives, Box 72: "Pasadena Art Institute." Ernest was president of the Pasadena Community Playhouse Association and his wife Alice Coleman was music director of the Coleman Concerts renamed the Coleman Chamber Music Association when it was incorporated in 1932.
14. *Pasadena Star-News*, July 5, 1929.
15. Joyce E. Pinney, comp., *A Pasadena Chronology, 1769-1977* (Pasadena: Pasadena Public Library, 1978), 118.
16. *Pasadena Star-News*, July 25, 1929.
17. For an account of the Civic Center competition, see Ann Scheid, *Pasadena: Crown of the Valley* (Northridge, Calif.: Windsor Publications, 1986), 133-36.
18. *Pasadena Star-News*, March 8, 1924.2. Pasadena Star-News, January 24, 1936.3. See Mary Davis MacNaughton, *Art at Scripps: The Early Years*, exh. cat. (Claremont, Calif.: Galleries of the Claremont Colleges, 1988), 16-17.
19. *Pasadena Star-News*, April 11, 1948.
20. Alan Batchelder, letter to the author, November 23, 1988.
21. *Pasadena Star-News*, April 11, 1948.
22. Alan Batchelder, letter to the author, November 23, 1988.

INDEX